Instructions for using AR

LET AUGMENTED REALITY CHANGE HOW YOU READ A BOOK

With your smartphone, iPad or tablet you can use the **Hasmark AR** app to invoke the augmented reality experience to literally read outside the book.

  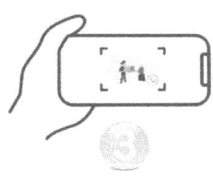

1. Download the **Hasmark app** from the **Apple App Store** or **Google Play**

2. Open and select the (vue) option

3. Point your lens at the full image with the and enjoy the augmented reality experience.

Go ahead and try it right now with the Hasmark Publishing International logo.

EQUILIBRIUM TODAY - BOOK 1

WORKING TOWARDS EQUILIBRIUM AFTER TRAUMA

Recovery from Sexual Abuse

INGOLFUR HARDARSON

Published by
Hasmark Publishing International
www.hasmarkpublishing.com

Copyright © 2024 Ingolfur Hardarson
First Edition

No part of this book may be reproduced or transmitted in any form or by any means, electronic or mechanical, including photocopying, recording or by any information storage and retrieval system, without written permission from the author, except for the inclusion of brief quotations in a review.

Disclaimer

This book is designed to provide information and motivation to our readers. It is sold with the understanding that the publisher is not engaged to render any type of psychological, legal, or any other kind of professional advice. The content of each article is the sole expression and opinion of its author, and not necessarily that of the publisher. No warranties or guarantees are expressed or implied by the publisher's choice to include any of the content in this volume. Neither the publisher nor the individual author(s) shall be liable for any physical, psychological, emotional, financial, or commercial damages, including, but not limited to, special, incidental, consequential or other damages. Our views and rights are the same: You are responsible for your own choices, actions, and results.

Permission should be addressed in writing to Ingolfur Hardarson at: info@equilibrium.today

Editor: Jamie Geidel   jamie@hasmarkpublishing.com
Cover Designer: Anne   Karklins anne@hasmarkpublishing.com
Interior Layout: Amit Dey   amit@hasmarkpublishing.com

ISBN 13: 978-1-77482-244-9
ISBN 10: 177482244X

DEDICATION

I was given this gift in early 2008. This gift gave me my life back and many others. This gift is not for me only; it is meant to be shared.

I am here to pay forward this gift and what I have learned since. I am trying to present it to you in the best manner that I can so you can apply its message to your life in the best way possible.

I dedicate this book to you.

I hope you find something in this book that will help you gain more clarity and peace in your life.

EPIGRAPH

Once we were born, we are here now. Something happened on our journey through life between those two milestones that are affecting us today. We need to find and work through them, heal our wounds, and get back up on the highway that is meant for our true, authentic life.

If I could, so can you. I believe in you!

ACKNOWLEDGMENTS

To my wonderful daughters, grandchildren, and sons-in-law. Thank you for putting up with me while I was stuck in consequential behavior patterns. Thank you for being so patient while I have been absent writing these books. You gave me a purpose to live. You saved my life.

Thanks to all of you who saw me, the true me, when I was stuck in my consequential behavior and did something about it. You who called me to check up on me and gave me information to work with. You who answered my calls any day, any time. Without you, I would not have realized where I was heading. You saved my life.

Thanks to all of you who have sought my assistance while working your way out of your darkness. You saved my life. Thanks to all of you who opened up to me with or without words, wanted to say something, and could not, yet you said so much. Without you all, I would not have healed as much as I have today. You are my inspiration to carry on with this journey.

Thanks to all of you who activated my emotional triggers connected to my trauma; you helped me to find the issues that I needed to address so my life could become better.

Thank you all at Hashmark Publishing, my tribe, for publishing these books. I could not have done it without you.

TABLE OF CONTENTS

Preface xvii

PART ONE: Awareness— What's in it for Me? . . . 1

   The State of Being: Fight, Flight, or Freeze. 13

   The Timeline 15

   The Emotional 24 Hours. 17

   What Options Do I Have?. 19

   The Responsibility that Creates Guilt which Leads
    to Shame and Feeling Dirty 21

   The Gender Issues Regarding "The Pain"
    and How We Deal with It. 27

   The Core of the Matter. 29

   Stepping into the Light and Telling Others. 33

   A Holistic Approach to Life 35

   Interaction with Others 37

   Our Self-Image and Dealing with Difficulty 39

   Better Not Do This Alone. 41

   Learned Behavior 43

Victim Of Violence As A Sexual Being In
  Relationships. 45
Subconscious Reminders 49
The Value of Personal Freedom 51
The Steppingstones
  to Personal Freedom 55
Self-Identity - The Ego Is More Like An App,
  Not An Operating System 59
Awareness of the Journey. 63

PART TWO: Understanding—The Key to Begin the Healing Process 65

What Is Going On? Why? Where Does the Pain
  Come From?. 67
Life's Journey 69
Where Does the Pain Come From? 73
Forgiveness—What Is It? 87
The Myth of Victims Becoming Abusers 91
Vocabulary about Sexual Abuse 93
It is often said that the truth cannot stand the light. . . 95
My Mental Dirt Pit 97
Internal Pain is good in its own nature.. 101
I did not die – I went into a coma state – I can
  get back!. 103
Just Anger or Justifiable Anger 105

- Categorizing Fear 107
- The Shaking of Coca-Cola® Syndrome. 109
- I love my so-called flaws..................... 113
- Wright Brothers Syndrome 115
- Present Defense Reflexes and Their Resistance to Change............................... 117
- The Infrastructure We Build Inside 119
- What Is Faith? Who or What Is My Higher Power? 121
- Operational Practices........................ 125
- Where Do You Want to Go?.................. 127
- The Formula for Happiness 139
- Emotional Volume and Dangerous Places........ 141
- Acts of Violence and Their Environment 151
- Addiction, Addicts, or Is It Something Else? 155
- Responsibility for the Emotional Responses of Others 161
- Before You Take on This Journey 163
- Additional Reading Material 171
- About the Author 173

TABLE OF FIGURES

Figure 1: The Big Picture. 4
Figure 2: The Layer We Are Addressing. 28
Figure 3: The Funnel of Consequential Behavior in
          the Now. 30
Figure 4: The Key Transformation 31
Figure 5: Steppingstones to Personal Freedom 56
Figure 6: The Big Picture 74
Figure 7: Violent Incident 76
Figure 8: Consequences. 78
Figure 9: Breaking Free 83
Figure 10: Dirt Pit. 99
Figure 12: Theory Merged into Life. 129
Figure 11: The Optimal Now 129
Figure 13: Healthy Life 130
Figure 14: The Need for Recognition Is Controlling
           Our Lives. 132
Figure 15: The Biological Threat 133

Figure 16: Risk-Needy 133
Figure 17: Love-, Sex-, Risk-Needy 134
Figure 18: Love- or Sex-Needy 134
Figure 19: Socially Needy 135
Figure 20: The Chaos Within 136
Figure 21: Today, after the Work. 137
Figure 22: Emotional Volume and Dangerous Places. . 142

PREFACE

Hello, welcome.

I am sorry to know that you have a reason to be here. At the same time, I want to assure you that there is always a solution to everything. We just need to find the right answers to our questions. If you do not find the answers you need when you are finished going through the material in this series of books, I urge you to keep on going. Never stop seeking. I am here because I got a gift back in early 2008, and now I am paying forward that gift and what I have learned since. Late in 2004, I started working on my issues related to mental, emotional, and physical abuse, and in late 2007 I started working on the sexual abuse that I endured as a kid. When I started to search for a solution for myself regarding sexual abuse, the conclusion was that there was none. I am a male, and back then service providers made no mention of men being sexually abused and, therefore, offered no solutions. The message was that it did not happen to me because of my gender. I knew better, so I had to figure it out. So here I am with my findings, and I hope you find it helpful.

There is one thing that I would like to emphasize! You are not a liar, loser, or anything else if you do not connect to everything in these books. Also, it does not mean that it did not happen to you though you do not fit into the content here. I can only give my perspective, and I know that I do not know everything. Everything evolves and matures, and it is highly likely that there will be new scenarios in this category in a few years. I can only do my best. Never forget that pain is pain, and consequences are consequences, and they are the roads to follow to heal our wounds and finally lead us to freedom from it all. Too often, simply categorizing something leads to discrimination. Let's try to stay out of that concept. That being said, I have to structure everything somehow but still keep an open mind.

I welcome you if you are here because you know somebody who endured sexual abuse. That tells me that you are a caring person, and you care for that person and want to do what you can to stand by that individual. It does not matter if it is a loved one, friend, coworker, or employee, or if you want to gain more knowledge regarding these issues. I know that you are a loving person, and I thank you for that. I also know that it is not easy to be with us when we fall into our wounds and the consequential behavior takes over. So, thank you for caring for us so much that you are here reading this book!

I welcome you if you are somewhere in our value chain of needs. First responders, police, medics, nurses, doctors, social workers, lawyers, judges, therapists, workers at recovery centers, volunteers, or students, I want to tell you that I am here to do what I can to help you help us. I am not here to take your place or to tell you what you should do. I am here to aid you in getting more understanding and to pay forward my knowledge about what we are going through and our functionality in our state of mind. *Equilibrium Today - Book 1 - Working Towards Equilibrium after Trauma* is about awareness of our life as a victim and preparations for the journey through recovery. *Equilibrium Today - Book 2 – Practical Tools for Equilibrium and Equilibrium Today - Book 3 – Recovery Workbook* are about starting the recovery journey and one of the ways to get out of victimhood and into personal freedom. After reading these books, I hope that you can add something to your tool chest to help us out of our state of mind. I am trying to bridge the gap between us. We need you! There are so many issues that arise through this process that we need you to help us through. I fully understand that taking the step toward us can be overwhelming. It is also overwhelming for us to take a step toward you—almost too much.

To those who are looking for healing, everything is possible when you put your mind and work into it. Everyone needs to find their own environment. It is a process, and there is no one correct answer for all. When that environment you found has returned maximum work and growth for you, considering what is offered there each time, you simply carry on and find another environment where the work and growth will continue. When you take on the journey of recovery I have laid out in these books and use the tools I have provided, and you walk through it to the end, if you still have some issues or answers you need to figure out, then, by all means, keep on going. Your answer is out there; you just have to find it. After all, it is accumulated knowledge and wisdom that will get you where you want to be.

There is only one thing that is not allowed. That is to give up. Defeat equals death!

My goal is to help at least one person to face life at its core and to become sustainable within—to build up an emotional tool chest that enables a person to take on life's adversities after sexual abuse and to know that nobody can reject you but yourself.

It is a journey from confinement to one's mental prison towards freedom and sustainability as an individual in one's own life, toward personal freedom in its most beautiful form. This is not an easy journey, but it is filled with personal victories on the way toward recovery and happiness. This is a little bit like sweet and sour. It is not possible to compare life before and after. It is simply unfair. The Now is so beautiful!

We can call it the transformation of the hidden Pain within that controls us. It is transformed from defensive responses, fight, flight, or freeze, into kind and loving responses when we are faced with challenging situations in life. This will lead us to an authentic life without fear.

The focus is on sexual abuse. But since sexual abuse includes all types of violence, you can use this methodology for all kinds of violence that occur in your life. Those of us who endure sexual violence do often have other violent experiences. After all, violence is violence, and consequences are consequences. Nothing can change that.

If your journey through the following content makes your life better in any way, then I am happy!

PART ONE

AWARENESS— WHAT'S IN IT FOR ME?

Let's dig in and look at the core of the matter.

You were born, and you are here today. Something happened in between. You need to find it, clean the wound that it created, heal it, care for it, listen to it, and work with it and the consequences that it created. You need to gain freedom from it in your life and step out and live.

I am going to tell you right now that you will not find any descriptions of violence or any names. This book only contains solution-oriented thoughts and tools that I and many others who sought my assistance have used for dealing with the consequences of being a victim of sexual violence. This content is about how we can feel awful when we are stuck in the consequential mindset of our experience and what we can do about it. There is a solution to everything.

The *amount* of violence does not matter since there will always be consequences. One time is too many, and consequences will always follow, whether it is one time or many! If you think that the violence you experienced was not significant enough or something along those lines, please do yourself a favor and throw that thought away. We have all been there—everybody! This way of thinking will do nothing for you and is entirely insignificant and useless. When I was a child, I experienced sexual violence, among other violent incidents, from outside of my family. It might seem trivial to compare my story to others, but thinking so will not help me. Comparing does not work; it does not deliver anything of value and is entirely useless. Violence is violence, and we will always need to deal with the consequences of that experience.

The consequences of violence stretch so far and so wide into your life as a victim that you need to deal with all the areas of being a human, no matter where or what. If I had to mention to what extent this experience did not affect me, I could only say my name and then walk away. Everything else ripples with consequences. We do not realize it until we start working on them and see and feel our lives again. Everything gets affected, unfortunately. The upside is that we will have a new beginning in our life, since we need to redefine ourselves, find the child within, and let it enjoy itself. We will become what we should have become and can become. It's about time.

We will have a possibility of a new life, so incredibly, ridiculously better than it was. My worst moment today is a thousand times better than my best moment before I went through this process. Life is so bright up ahead that you almost must wear sunglasses. But when we get used to the brightness, we take down the sunglasses and enjoy the light. It does not mean that it will be easy. No way! This journey is challenging, and I am not going to sugarcoat it. I can promise that the triumphs on the way are amazing, so it is not all bad. Do not miss out on them. Enjoy the victories; they will fuel you to more accomplishments.

Some of the issues and tools in this book will be useful to meditate on for a while. Everything here is important for the recovery process. Some of the concepts need to be read and digested many times, over and over. It's okay; this is your recovery, and the only amount of time, number of recurrences, and speed that is needed is what suits you. *Your* speed is the only right speed: your healing, your responsibility. At the same time, it is important not to exceed your limitations. Nobody can do this for you. Nobody can tell you what is right for you. The answer is always within you, and it is up to you to find it.

The overall process from the infliction to freedom can be divided into three segments, as the picture below shows.

4 Working Towards Equilibrium After Trauma

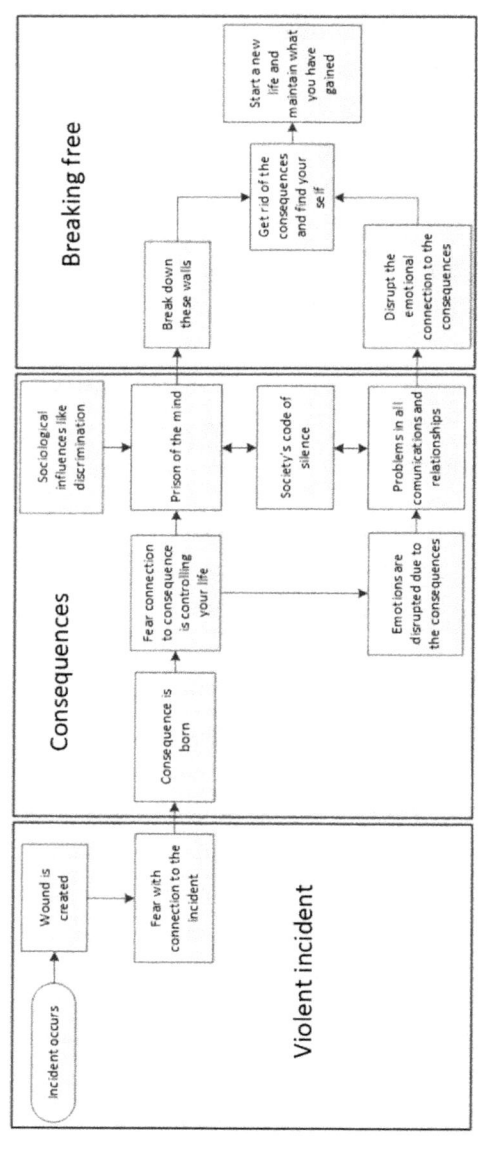

Figure 1: The Big Picture

One of the most challenging things we will have to cope with is love and kindness. We do not fully know how to handle it and what we should do with it. Kindness and love often came before violent incidents happened to us in the past. That is why it can provoke protective reflexes within us today. We must learn to trust love and kindness all over again, in the right way.

The second issue is anger. What is anger? How do we go about expressing it? We can feel helpless in front of this emotion. It can be related to the responses from others when we tell them about the violence that we endured. It can result in our not knowing how to deal with that emotion. We cannot express or let out the injustice we encountered. It is boiling underneath the surface, and we do not know how to handle it. This can lead to explosive responses to others on a scale that does not fit the circumstances. Sometimes we think that our explosive responses are anger, and that can lead to our being afraid to be angry. Explosive responses are not anger—they are simply explosions of the buried pain and injustice that we endured during and after the abuse occurred in our lives. We must learn what anger is and how it functions without the wounds.

I mention Higher Power a lot. I call mine the Divine Power; you will find your own definition. I chose it because the name does not connect to fear within me. I found the words *Lord* or *God* too overpowering—words leading to submission, which I do not like. Never again. This is just my choice, and you choose yours. My Divine Power is above religion. It is the love and light of the universe that shines and embraces everything. Religion, for me, is more like a lifestyle. Where we are in that area has more to do with where we are born, where we live, and which religion governs each society. We are all equal. I think all of us have faith differing only in what we choose to believe in. Everyone has his or her beliefs, which is a good thing. The big issue here is that we need to be connected to something higher than ourselves that we can trust and that gives us unconditional love. Something to which we can give our secrets. Something that is in direct contact with our inner being, always, every day. There is no person who can fulfill this role for me, just my Higher Power. If you are against it, try finding something that suits you while going through this process, and you can always give it up when you are done.

The great thing about it all is that there is no roof over happiness. There is a roof to being unhappy. That roof is our bottom, which we cannot go beyond. Amazingly, bottoms have three main benefits. First, they make a great platform to stand up from, a solid foundation. The second is that everything is upward from that point. The third is that something died inside of us that was not working and did not work for our benefit. By letting this concept die, it creates space for something new that benefits us more. But happiness itself does not have a roof. Happiness will continue to grow, which is amazingly beautiful. If you go through the process and keep growing and maturing, happiness will continue to grow within you. When there, then the only thing you need to do is to keep on doing what you are doing, and happiness will follow proportionately to your own growth. Life can be so beautiful.

There will be moments when you will be exhausted, which is normal. It takes a lot of energy from your bodily system to process your emotions. Do not beat yourself up. Allow yourself to be tired and take the time to rest. After all, the brain is the organ that takes up the most energy of all.

What is this book series all about?

Equilibrium Today - Book 1 - Working Towards Equilibrium after Trauma (This book)

In Part One, "Awareness," you will get a better insight into the life of a victim of sexual abuse. Remember that though we are victims, it does not mean we have to live like one. I am a victim, but I refuse to live like one. I will not live in the vortex of consequential behavior. The violence left me in a fight, flight, or freeze response. To get out of that state, I must work on my issues to gain my freedom again.

In Part Two, "Understanding," you will get insight into the journey ahead. There are so many issues that we are not aware of before we start to look into our life after a violent incident that we endured. I will discuss issues and concepts that we need to address and have in mind before we take on the journey ahead. It will help us understand the effects of being a victim of sexual abuse on our lives. Understanding is key to being able to get out of the vortex of fight, flight, or freeze states of mind. Never forget, it is a consequential behavior, not you! It does not define you, but it defines what you need to work on. It helps you to put a face on the consequences. If we cannot see and hear what we are dealing with then it is impossible to work on it. The better you understand what you are dealing with, the faster you process it all.

Equilibrium Today - Book 2 – Practical Tools for Equilibrium and Equilibrium Today - Book 3 – Recovery Workbook

The chapter "Mapping and Processing" is about getting control over today's issues. To be in the present and to reach inner peace, to stay in the moment, in the Now. You will start to gain control over tools that will lead your emotional states to solutions. These tools will help free you from the pain and show you how to live in love and kindness no matter what the situation is at hand. Using these tools will release you from the rapid emotional turmoil that has too much influence and control over your life.

In the chapter "Connecting the dots," you see the connections in your behavioral patterns. You see the relationship between cause and effect and how consequences have globally ruled your life. Everything starts to make sense, and you start understanding how much influence the consequences have on all aspects of your life. You will also see, as you conquer your fear, no matter how it presents itself, how conquering fear solves other issues in your life. There seems to be a core connection underneath that affects all our life in a way, like common ground. It will be as if you get access to fuel lines that have been feeding fires all over your life, and you get ready to cut off the access of these fuel lines into your life just by turning one handle. Fear will no longer rule your life.

When we get to the chapter "Leaving the chaos," we have mapped our consequential behavior and connected the dots regarding how all this is related to our lives today. With all this understanding, we can start to walk away from the chaos that we were unable to see, understand, and manage. The actual steps toward our personal freedom are in progress.

"Letting go" discusses how to let go of control issues—the control that was governed by fear, shame, tearing yourself down, and was, in fact, violence against yourself.

You will learn how to give control to your Higher Power which can be characterized by love and kindness in all things, especially towards yourself, and by that, to others at the same time.

"Being whole again" is about reconnecting with the whole part of ourselves. We were born once, and we are here today. Something happened in between that time. We have found it and are working through the trauma, healing it, and starting to become healthy again—regaining the healthy part of ourselves. With the understanding, knowledge, and tools we have built up so far, we are able to reconnect to the healthy part without falling back into fight, flight, or freeze behavior. It is a journey, and there will be ups and downs, but it is okay. We are standing up again, and when we have been lying down under the consequences for a long time, it will take some time to regain our balance.

"More Memory Surfaces" will emerge when we open the door to allow memories to come up to the surface, then it is like we are breaking down a water dam. In the beginning, a little bit of water starts seeping. As our ability to handle the memories and what comes with them starts to rise, more water comes down. In the end, the dam is not there anymore, and water flows freely down the memory lane. In the end, there are no secrets that are taking you to the grave, you are free!

"Cleaning Up" ensures that you keep what you have earned. You will learn how to take accountability for the things in the past. You will learn how to be accountable for yourself, how you can do it today, every day, always, and you will learn that freedom is the result of accountability. If you do not become accountable, your past will come back and beat you to the ground. Everything will go back to square one, and you will have to do the process all over again to get going again.

The "New Me" is about living in the recovery that you achieved in this process. These are the tools of maintenance, the tools you have learned to use and applied to your life so far. Each of us puts together our own version of the tools that work for each of us to deal with what life has brought us in our everyday life. You will find discussions on issues and concepts that hopefully will help you figure out what suits you in your life. Never forget that it is your life, and you implement what fits you and your views towards how to live your life. I am not telling you that you must do this and that! I am not your guru, you are!

THE STATE OF BEING: FIGHT, FLIGHT, OR FREEZE

We talk about three stages that we fall into: fight, flight, or freeze.

Fight state is when we fight the opponent to get free from the abusive situation.

Flight state is when we flee the opponent to get out of abusive situations.

Freeze is when we go into a kind of paralyzed, immobile state of our body. We are unable to move, say, or do anything. The way I understand it is that the natural opioids within our body numb us in the manner that we disconnect from our body and feel no bodily pain but at the same time we are fully alert.

There is ongoing research; more definitions and clarifications will emerge in the future. Keep informed by searching the Internet.

THE TIMELINE

How long does it take? That is a very relative concept. It varies based on each of us. How long ago was the violent act committed on you? How robust is the current coping mechanism? What have you done so far? And more factors. Take a look at your life. You are here. That means you are a solution-oriented person. You are strong. You are clever. Also, take a look at what you have done so far. I am pretty sure that you have done a lot. You have been reading, searching, and all of that is what you stand on today. You will get through this based on your qualities, knowledge, wisdom, and what you have done so far. Do not throw away what you have done so far and your accumulated knowledge of today. Everything is correct in the universe. Everything happens for a reason, although we cannot see that at each given time.

We are all different, and there is no time frame righter than yours. It is all right! Time will pass anyway. You are here and adding to your knowledge and arsenal. That is time well spent and shortens the total recovery time. You cannot speed things up beyond your capabilities. It can be dangerous. The only thing that matters is getting home again and gaining inner peace.

THE EMOTIONAL 24 HOURS

Our emotional 24 hours is in fact 12 months. It is like you must go through an entire year, create new norms in that time and eliminate the old ones. Summer holiday, Christmas, Easter, birthdays, etcetera. The first year is strange, the next one is better, and then life is amazing. I am making new norms for next year every day; it is up to me how they will turn out. The consequential behavior is based on conditioning, and this journey will break up these conditions, and you will set a new one that will benefit you for the rest of your life.

Sometimes, when going through a rough period in our lives, it can be good to think ahead of today into the future. Where do we want to be after this turbulent period? Not to escape the Now, but to create a new foundation to stand on when it is over.

You can start changing your future today even though today is not so good. Be in the Now and decide that a year from now, I will be in a great place in all aspects of my life! Apply your knowledge, ability, and mental tools to take on what is in front of you. Add mental tools to help you acquire that goal. Make new references for your last emotional 24 hours and smile!

Amazingly, our body renews itself about 96-98% each year. There seems to be a universal law in place.

WHAT OPTIONS DO I HAVE?

There are two options: do nothing or take on the journey. We always make progress, no matter what we choose. If we decide to do nothing, we will progress downward into more darkness and pain. If we decide to do the work, walk into the pain, sit down with it, listen to what it has to say, and do something about it, then we progress upward. For me, I was at a crossroads. Either I talked and worked on my issues, or I would end my life. I could not make it anymore; I could not live like that anymore. Here I am! It was not easy, but totally worth it!

THE RESPONSIBILITY THAT CREATES GUILT WHICH LEADS TO SHAME AND FEELING DIRTY

As a victim of violence, you will take Responsibility for the act if there is something that you sought in the environment related to the violent act you endured.

In the beginning stages before the violent act occurred, if you wanted something—anything—from the violator, the situation, or something related to the environment leading up to the act, it can create a thinking process that has nothing to do with reality. This thinking process emerges after the violence started that made you feel responsible.

For example:

I chose to go to that place, I talked to this person, I let this individual into my home, I had a warm thought about this person, etcetera.

Was I responsible for that? I must be, since I chose to interact with this individual. Yes, but I went there and should have known better. I am ashamed of myself.

During it all comes the feeling that I am unclean, full of disgusting feelings, that I am dirty.

If we break it down, then this process emerges.

The process:

I chose this because of "something," and I got abused.

With "my choosing" comes the feeling of Responsibility.

Guilt is created as a by-product of this Responsibility.

It brings Shame into the picture.

Being Unclean wanders around and pops up at various or all steps of the process.

These things will only bring you chaos made by the violator, who likes to keep you there. You get stuck in a vortex of this Responsibility, Guilt, and Shame over something that you did not instigate nor create in the first place—feeling unclean along the way.

You are never responsible for being violated—never! You just happened to be there. If it had not been you, then it would have been someone else. That means that there was nothing personal about it. You just happened to be there.

There is nothing to feel guilty about. Nothing. You did not ask for violations. Somebody made the decision; it was not your choosing!

There is nothing you need to feel ashamed of. It was not a bad judgment on your behalf, and you could not have done better.

That feeling of being Unclean has nothing to do with you. It is not yours; it belongs to your violator. This person left this with you, tried to smear it all over you, get it inside you so that it will control your life, take you down, and let you feel unworthy of existence. It will not matter how much you clean yourself because it will not go away until you work through the trauma. Remember always—you are not the dirty one!

You are a pure, clean, and beautiful soul and a lovely human being. You are traumatized and have consequences, and it does not define you in any way.

I felt Responsible for everything because I did not get any help around the violence that I endured. There was nothing in my environment that reflected to me that what happened was wrong in any way. I was alone with it all and with all my thoughts, so it must have been my fault. It never is!

My story is that I wandered around in this existence, lost, violated, and it was hidden from me. The memories were locked down. I tried to find peace, fell into this and that, this relationship and that, bouncing out because they were not suitable for me; my inner being was lost. I took responsibility for everything that got in my way. Not just for having peeked into this room or that existence, but for the room itself and the existence of it. I felt like it was my choosing to be there and all that nonsense.

The fact is that I am only responsible for having peeked, but nothing else. Having shouldered this crazy Responsibility is directly connected to the Responsibility planted in me after the violence I encountered. The connection was the violent act, and everything related to it.

All of this was hidden from me, and I carried issues for which I did not know what they were or what to do with them—being ridiculously miserable, feeling pain, Guilt, Responsibility, Shame, and Uncleanliness that was not mine. But now I am out of this vortex. I am free. I am my own master and shoulder my own Responsibility—only mine, not others'.

Nothing of this belongs to you. It is not yours! The violator, and no one else, owns it all and will thrive if you feel like this. They want you to think like that because then you are more likely to maintain the silence.

You can only do one thing with Responsibility, Guilt, Shame, and Dirt, and that is to throw them away. They are not yours. They were never yours in the beginning, and you have nothing to do with them.

Working through the trauma makes you capable of throwing the Responsibility, Guilt, Shame, and Dirt out with the trash.

It feels so good to take out the trash! Do not miss out on it!

THE GENDER ISSUES REGARDING "THE PAIN" AND HOW WE DEAL WITH IT

There are many discussions regarding whether there is a difference between genders regarding effects of sexual abuse. There seems to be more focus on the differences between us instead of what unites us. What I have learned is that the core root of the pain we are dealing with is below the gender layer of our being. I have noticed that consequences are gender-neutral, meaning that it does not matter what type of body you were born in.

Let us lay down any thoughts about gender relations while going through this process. It is at later stages, after we have gone through all the material I can provide here, that the difference of gender comes into play. At its core, we cannot genderize feelings, pain, fear, and fight, flight, or freeze responses. The core focus is on the core emotional layer before discussing gender layers.

There is a danger of discriminating against somebody by categorizing this level of emotions as gender issues. When we are done digging up the debris from the abuse and have gathered our core emotional being, and we are standing upright in our life, ready to walk into our common society, then we can start to approach matters gender-wise, whatever gender you belong to. That is an entirely different matter and approach. I will not go into that space.

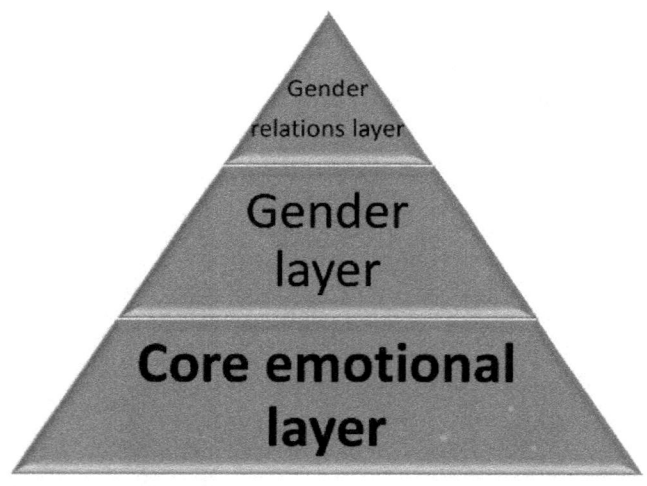

Figure 2: The Layer We Are Addressing

Let's stand together, support each other! Focus on our common denominators! We are all one! We are all awesome!

Love and kindness triumph over all!

THE CORE OF THE MATTER

We objectify ourselves as human beings.

We are no longer members of the species homo sapiens, humankind.

We personalize the consequential behavior as being us because we have lost sight of who we truly are. We must reverse this role. We must personalize ourselves again and objectify the consequential behavior to break free and get our life back.

Truth guided by love and kindness conquers all. I have faith in you!

Where is the key component that needs to change in the chain of emotional response?

If we dive into the core of the transformation that has to take place, then the pictures illustrate it as I understand it. We must learn to see the chaos within and make it tangible. Get to know it. Learn what it means. Learn and practice to get a grip on it. Learn and understand what is behind it. Heal what we find. Learn to change our emotional responses due to what we find. Practice and get fluent in moving our emotional responses over to love and kindness responses—by doing that, we will also treat others the same way.

By accomplishing this, you will start to gain control of your emotional responses, the first step out of consequential responses that control our entire emotional life. The vortexes will start to lose control over you.

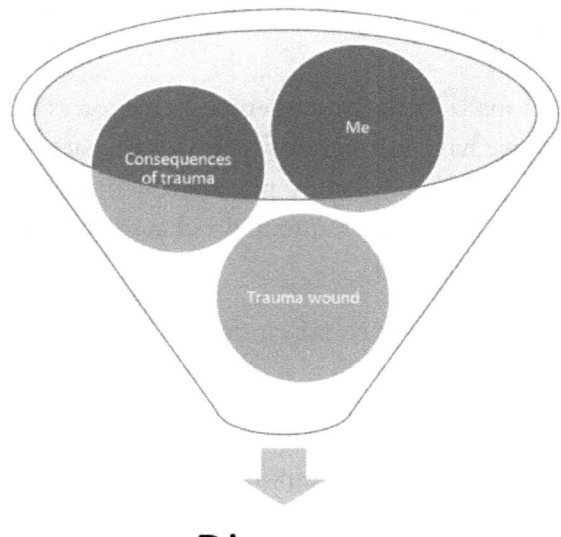

Figure 3: The Funnel of Consequential Behavior in the Now

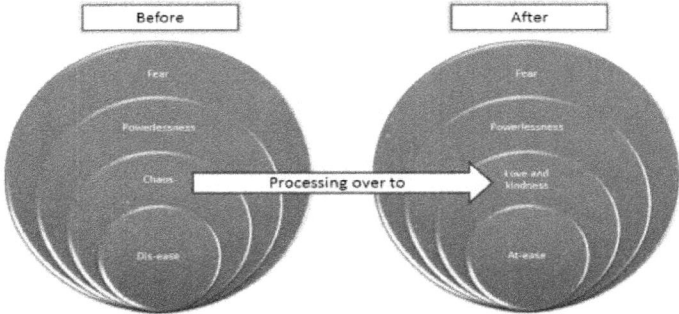

Figure 4: The Key Transformation

STEPPING INTO THE LIGHT AND TELLING OTHERS

Considering how society has functioned throughout time, the repercussions of disclosing having been a victim of sexual abuse have been enormous for us. That alone has kept victims and their families in the darkness of silence and has led to unmentionable pain for these individuals. This has been the optimal situation for offenders because it is precisely what they rely on and thrive in, since silence protects them but kills the victims. I believe this is mainly done unconsciously, and I refuse to believe that there is a conscious evil behind it.

We often say that we have a problem when the truth comes out into the light, that the truth cannot handle the light. There is a quote that says, "It's our light, not our darkness, that most frightens us." Here in Iceland, we say, "The truth cannot withstand the daylight."

I think that there is a little bit of misunderstanding in that. I think people have issues with the ugliness that follows the truth. We need to strengthen ourselves to face what comes with the truth and gain strength in working through it, accepting it with love. That does not just relate to this issue, but everything. Silence guards secrets that cause pain, which maintains the pain. This, again, is bad for society, and we need to stop maintaining that loop.

Love conquers all, and we need to address problems with love and kindness. To destroy darkness, you only need to turn on the light, the light of love, and everybody will feel better. This light can hurt your eyes the first time it is turned on, but then our eyes will adjust to it. We must do that—adjust to what we see and work through it. Life will be more beautiful, and the pain will subside and finally go away. Every time we tell our story, we will remove one stone from the prison, the brick wall that we have built around us, one brick at a time.

A HOLISTIC APPROACH TO LIFE

The human body is truly a remarkable organism that, with great accuracy, detects when something is right or wrong in our reality. When finding a fault in the system, it swiftly takes action to bring it to our awareness. That might manifest itself through body aches, emotional turmoil, and obsessive, unproductive, or negative thoughts. Awareness, or being totally aligned with our inner being, is thus the crucial key for a healthy, happy, balanced life. Nevertheless, the road to awareness doesn't come that easy to all of us. A traumatic background usually teaches us that the safest way to survive is to detach from our bodies, whereas coming from a relatively peaceful environment makes us more prone to become mindful of our body signals and act accordingly.

INTERACTION WITH OTHERS

After constantly working on myself, my conversations with others about any topic or life in general have become more consistent and in accordance with who I actually am. Before starting this work, the answers were a bit scattered and inconsistent to my core being, probably because I did not know myself that much at the time. I did not know myself all the way to the core of my being, but I reacted to the best of my ability each time. I did my best.

Is it honest when you look into the rearview mirror, applying today's knowledge, capabilities, and personal growth through the years, to criticize your decisions and actions made back in time? I do not think so. If I beat myself up for the past, then I am actually doing a violent act toward myself. The only thing that I can do is learn from it and try to do better in the future. Violence in close relationships is forbidden, including toward myself.

Constantly answering criticism about your life can develop into justifying your existence. Justifying that you can and have the right to be here on this Earth among other fellow human beings.

I was constantly setting up my life to control the emotional environment that I lived in—answering and trying to foresee and control the outcome in every situation that was in front of me, which was not a good place to be in. In these situations, I was in a fight, flight, or freeze state—not good—fighting for, fleeing from, or emotionally frozen in my existence.

When we come from a traumatized situation, there can be abnormalities to what we put into the danger category. We have put communication, love and kindness, and interaction with others into the danger category. That is clearly an abnormal reaction to normal situations when there is no clear or present danger. We must stop justifying our existence, work on the fear of the unknown, and make space for ourselves in the world. We have as much right to be here as any other! Recategorizing is necessary—we must put communication, love, kindness, and interaction and reaction with others into a more loving and kinder category.

OUR SELF-IMAGE AND DEALING WITH DIFFICULTY

I am going to draw you a picture of one way to look at difficulty based on low self-image.

Let's imagine that we as individuals are all the same height but that we stand at different heights in the difficulty jungle, depending on how strong our self-image is. Our self-image is our height support; we are lifted higher when it is strong than when it is crumbling.

If your self-image is big and strong, the obstacles in the difficulty jungle can be easily overcome. We can see over them. I can get over this and that. I see that there is something called "the other side of the difficulties in the jungle."

If your self-image is broken, if the support is low, and you cannot see over the difficulties in the difficulty jungle, you are lost. You tell yourself: *I cannot do this. I cannot see that there is a point in plowing through this jungle. There is nothing on the other side; I cannot see it anyway. It is just supposed to be like this. Okay. I will just stay here. Life is probably supposed to be like this.*

It is like the old Icelandic saying: "If you get lost in an Icelandic forest, you only have to stand up." Your self-image needs to be built up so that you have the strength to see over your problems and see that it is all right. There is a light at the end of the tunnel. You are here, so you are on your way. I believe in you!

BETTER NOT DO THIS ALONE

It is very important to get someone with you when you take on this journey. No one goes through an experience like this alone. If you decide to take this step and work through the process until you are free from the consequences, bring someone you trust with you. It can be someone with the same experience as yours, and you support each other through it, or it can be someone else. Do not go through it alone, as it can be dangerous. You need someone to talk to when the mountains that you are trying to climb seem to be too high.

There will be issues that come up during this journey, and I recommend that you seek professional help with these issues without interfering with the process itself. If you are not ready to expose what you are going through at the moment, then you can take individual issues to the therapist and work through them. You can tell the therapist when you are ready. If you do not want to do it, then that is okay too. It is your life.

The best thing that our closest person can do is to help us with our emotions and daily functions of things that are called life. It's not to tell us what to do but to help us sort out what these are and how to use them, to help us with functionality in life—clarifications and definitions of things and how to apply them. Dear closest one, do not take it personally if we fall into our wounds and have a hard time getting back up from them. Our emotional reactions can be very mixed and hard to read. This is just an outburst of suppressed emotions. This is a consequential behavior, nothing more—a fight, flight, or freeze state of mind.

At the same time, we have to keep in mind that being in that state is an explanation, not an excuse. At some point during this process, I recommend that our loved ones seek help regarding working through emotional issues that have arisen during their time living with us.

LEARNED BEHAVIOR

We have learned how to survive. To do that, we have learned a particular behavior. In fact, we had a normal response to an abnormal situation during the trauma period. Then when we walk out into our life and are no longer in the trauma period, our responses become abnormal responses to normal situations.

You did everything right in order to survive, and without these responses, you might not be reading these lines. Let's rejoice in your being here to read them.

The good news is that since it is a learned behavior, it means that you can also unlearn it and learn new responses without the behavior pattern of your past trauma.

Many people out there do not know that what was done to them was wrong. Life is not working, and they do not know why, suffering alone and blaming themselves for everything that is dysfunctional in their lives. I am glad you are here!

VICTIM OF VIOLENCE AS A SEXUAL BEING IN RELATIONSHIPS

There is no wonder that victims of violence have problems in relationships, especially close ones.

Loving someone when that person has the same bodily tools used in a crime of violence against you will often lead to mixed feelings for that someone you love. It does not matter that you or your lover has these tools. It will usually be a love-hate relationship until you have worked through the consequences of the violence. It has nothing to do with your current lover; it is all within you. If you are in an abusive relationship, then that is another topic—get out of it ASAP!

If the abuser is of the other sex than the victim, and the victim's lover is of the same sex as the abuser, it can be difficult for the victim to look at their lover. The victim can be thinking of their past memories and treat their current lover from that difficult place.

Where the victim is of the same sex as the abuser, the victim can find it is tough to feel like a sexual being. To have the same equipment as was being used against you will lead to disgust and rejection of yourself.

You can oscillate between "Do not touch me!" and "Come here!" One moment you let yourself off the leash and say "Come here," and the next moment, "Go away," and then "Come," then "Go away" which can happen again and again.

You will have to work hard to feel comfortable with yourself.

For our lovers, it is tough to be around us when we are in constant conflict with our sexuality and the way we look at our lovers. Our lovers might think that we are having an affair. By the way, that is a normal reaction to our behavioral process. We are emotionally distant, not because we are not in love with that person, but we are stuck in our wounds. The sooner we get free from it all, the better!

We have to take responsibility for what is going on inside of our emotional being and tell our lover why. Otherwise, we will lose our lover, and the relationship will break apart for all the wrong reasons. I had many relationships that got into conflict for these reasons and broke apart for all the wrong reasons. It took me many years and hard work to realize what actually happened and why my lovers thought I was having an affair when I adored my lover each time. Keep in mind that when you are reflecting on past relationships, treat it with care, love, and kindness toward yourself. You, just like me, did not have a chance to be in a healthy relationship. We did not have the capacity to do so. We were stuck in our wounds at that time and were not capable of functioning properly. We must process these encounters and go through the grieving process to let go of them.

If I could do it, so can you! I believe in you!

SUBCONSCIOUS REMINDERS

It seems like the reason our subconscious mind maintains our memories, or clues to them, is to make sure the issues will get resolved. Memories are the pathway to the wounds that were created during the abuse. To heal, we must follow this pathway to clean and heal the wound. It is a good idea to write down the memories or clues to them, and keep them in a safe place. This will help them to leave our heads and stop disturbing our daily life. Our subconscious mind can relax, knowing that these issues will be resolved. We do not have to work fully on them at that moment, but writing short notes about them loosens the grip they have on us.

THE VALUE OF PERSONAL FREEDOM

Many of us go through our lives without understanding the concept of personal freedom. Sadly, too often we confuse societal freedom with personal freedom without ever questioning the core of it, let alone how personal freedom can change the course of our lives for the better when consciously exercised on a daily basis.

The concept of personal freedom is a joint phrase involving two very important key words—person and freedom. Let us examine further the fundamental levels of this concept.

First, it means that we as human beings are free to have and develop our very own independent thoughts and views regarding everything that we experience in life.

Second, we are free to develop into the unique individuals that we are always becoming, given that we never stop learning more about ourselves as we go along on our journey of life.

Third, we are free to have our independent ideas about how we want to live our lives and to live life on our terms.

Fourth, we are free to have our independent opinions and attitudes regarding everything that our life entails.

Fifth, we are free to pursue all activities that evoke our interest, social or economic, as long as they do not inflict harm on another. Here we are taking the step into social freedom.

For a long time or a little over four decades, I wandered around with only a trivial understanding of the meaning of the concept of personal freedom. For a large extent of that time, it was not unusual for me to find myself in situations that did not in any way serve my highest good as a free individual human being. On the contrary, quite early on in life, I learned that there was very little space in my immediate environment for personal freedom.

Instead of evolving as free individuals in our lives, in many ways, we become the antonym of the concept. In other words, we become slaves. Slaves to the expectations of others. Our existence thus becomes highly dependent on how others value us rather than the other way around—valuing ourselves. The harder we try to conform to the expectations of others, the more we lose the inner connection to ourselves. The more we lose our inner connection, the less we begin to value ourselves, until looking into the mirror we feel we are looking at a stranger. This is what I experienced, and it is a vicious cycle in which many of us become utterly stuck, some even for a whole lifetime. Imagine spending an entire lifetime enslaved by the expectations of others, sitting on the sidelines of your own life, always waiting for the next beckoning.

When that day arrived that I was finally able to grasp the real essence of this concept and became mindful of how I could transform my life through this instrumental concept, I was at last able to take full control of my life back into my own hands, where it belongs. This tool is consequently a worthy one to keep handy in your mental toolbox.

THE STEPPINGSTONES TO PERSONAL FREEDOM

Now let us go through the steps that take us to personal freedom, to the most inner strength. One step at a time. To be in a relationship with ourselves first and foremost makes us able to be in relationships with other people, such as love relationships, friendships, and other relationships that are significant for our life.

One of the obstacles we have to go through is to find where to begin—what is the first step, the right place to start to work up the ladder to emotional freedom and sustainability in life.

So, let's take a walk.

The Right to Exist

In our opinion, we often feel like we do not have the right to exist in our own lives. We often feel like we are excluded. We often think others would be much better off if we were not here. This does not reflect the will of

56 Working Towards Equilibrium After Trauma

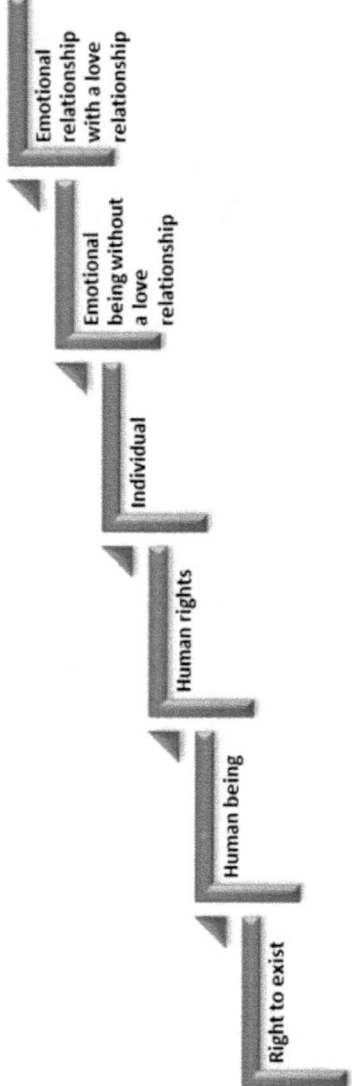

Figure 5: Steppingstones to Personal Freedom

the nation. This is a state of mind that is a fact to *us*, but thankfully it does not reflect reality. We need to get out of this state of mind and claim our right to exist.
Human Being

We feel like we are at the end of the food chain, like something undefined that does not fit in. We are not a part of the human race. We need some sort of connection to the rest of humanity to be included in everyday life.

Human Rights

We feel like we do not have the right to exist in this life, that we are nothing. We do not belong with others. We often feel like everybody else is higher in the food chain than us. We need to claim the right to belong to the human race, to take our space, to be included, and to have the same rights as others.

Individuality

We need to get to be individuals in our lives—independent beings with needs and desires—and to elevate it to be a normal state of mind for us. We need to gain individual freedom, to be a free individual in our own life. To be an active and sustainable participant in life in unity with others with self-respect and take up room as such an individual.

Emotional Being without a Love Relationship

We need to connect with ourselves to get to know our emotions and live with them in equilibrium. Our emotions are in a chaotic state that we do not know how to handle. We need to learn how to handle our emotions and how to use them to communicate with others.

Emotional Life with a Love Relationship

We need to handle existing as an emotional being in love and simultaneously as an independent and active individual in our own lives. We do not need to please others to be accepted and do not interpret kindness as love or sex as love. We need to learn how to handle the emotions of love without being sidetracked in other aspects of our life. This is the highest state of being.

SELF-IDENTITY - THE EGO IS MORE LIKE AN APP, NOT AN OPERATING SYSTEM

The ego is probably the biggest part of our foundation, not the operating system. It is more like an app than anything else—a manuscript, but not a published book.

If we use the analogy of traveling, then we could say that the ego is the GPS equipment. We have the gadget and then we need to fill it with information and take care of its operational uptime. We put maps into it, we put in the coordinates of our traveling path, we make sure that it has electricity or charge, we connect it to the internet to make sure that the settings are right according to the magnetic field around the Earth. When everything is in place, we push the button and go on a journey. How we use it is what we can call the intuition. We know that it is not 100% accurate. We must take in the environment. We must compensate when the Northern lights are strong because there is a fluctuation in the Earth's magnetic field when they are strong. Even in some places on the planet no navigation equipment works. For example, close to the craters of the volcano Eyjafjallajökull, the volcano that grounded air traffic in Europe in 2010, neither compasses nor GPS work. Then we are operating in the intuition state, and the journey will be successful.

We must constantly update the GPS equipment for the reference to Earth's magnetic field, the maps, regular maintenance, and more. You can also look at it as your CV, the accumulated knowledge and experience that is constantly updated but does not rule your everyday life.

The ego is constantly growing in a cognitive manner, we are constantly learning and growing, and that is great. Otherwise, we are stuck in the past, and life becomes dull and predictable.

We need our ego to stand on as a foundation, not to operate from on a daily basis. If we do not know who we are, then we are in a fairly bad place, with a lost or dysfunctional ego.

Lost Ego

If we come from a turbulent past, we need to figure our selves out to have something to stand on as an individual and a person; sometimes we have lost who we are. We need to build up our ego so we can have structure, a structure that we are content with that makes us strong in a loving and kindly manner. We must be able to be vulnerable while we are strong. It is essential for our structure and our strategic plan while traveling through life.

Functional Ego

When we are happy with who we are and what we stand for, then we can let go of the ego. We need to maintain it in a structure that we are happy in without being egocentric, rather just pure peace and love standing strong in ourselves. Keep in mind that we have to maintain the ego when needed.

Transition into Intuition

When we are strong in the ego that we are happy with, then we can take the next step towards our freedom and happiness. The next step is to let the intuition take over and let it rule the flow of life. I do not need the ego in front of me traveling through life anymore. It is there and has an extremely important role, not as a governing tool in my daily life but as a foundation that I stand on as a person.

Operating Our Daily Life from Intuition

Intuition is amazing! It allows me to be in the flow and not afraid of what life brings me. I have built up my mental toolbox that I place in the egosystem that reacts when something comes into my life that needs to be dealt with. The intuition brings me scenarios that broaden my life—some things that are new to me—and my life experience and understanding increases. That is so wonderful! I get to grow and develop every day as a human being, and best of all, I get a pleasant surprise factor of many interesting aspects of life that I did not know about.

AWARENESS OF THE JOURNEY

There is a great journey ahead. It will be difficult, and that is all right. If this work does not hit you hard, you are not doing it right. If you do not feel hurt, if you do not cry because of the pain, sorrow, love, and joy, if you do not scream or laugh, feel the rage burn inside so that you feel like you are about to explode or implode, then you are not dealing entirely with the wounds inside of you. After all, it is about evoking emotions buried inside since the time we were traumatized—turning them on instead of having them in coma mode and feeling nothing.

You may get a little extreme while working through these issues, but that is all right. You will balance it out again, and life will be amazing. You are actually getting out your real emotions, but the thing is that we do not know how they work or how to use them. In some cases, we have even never used them in the way they were intended for us. It will take time to get to know them, which is all right. Time will pass anyway, so take all the time you need. We need to learn how we function, how our responses work, how we interpret things, how we process things, what we do, and how we communicate with others about what we are experiencing. We need to learn how to trust these newer or hardly-used functions, know our emotions, and live by them.

I need to realize that my points of reference do not work. I cannot use my reflections on my own life; they are unreliable. If they were reliable, I would not have pain inside while reading this text and taking on this journey.

One of the first things we learn is to intervene in the right place in the right way. The point to intervene is where Powerlessness starts. Until now, most reflexes have come from Chaos, but now we learn that we can have a choice. We acquire the ability and capacity to choose what to do with the feeling of being Powerless. We can choose the path of Love and Kindness instead of Chaos, and then life becomes more beautiful. Working with Powerlessness gives us tools to figure out what is really bothering us.

Here is some additional reading material to help your awareness:

The blog: https://equilibrium.today/

Search the Internet for everything that comes to mind. I searched how to brush teeth, and my life became better.

PART TWO

UNDERSTANDING—THE KEY TO BEGIN THE HEALING PROCESS

WHAT IS GOING ON? WHY? WHERE DOES THE PAIN COME FROM?

Understanding is the key to knowledge, and you can progress that into wisdom. The best part is that if you understand something, then you do not have to remember that something. It is in your wisdom base.

I will try to paint you a picture of the spectrum that our life is all about when we fall into our consequential behavior. Bear with me; there is a point to it all. This journey is about getting back up on our feet again in synchronicity with our inner being and seeing what life has to offer. That includes living in equilibrium with our own social and work life, or any other aspect of life.

LIFE'S JOURNEY

Life is a fantastic journey. All of us are looking for love and kindness in our lives. We are always trying to be better, have more, and feel better than last year—more than the others, more than that guy or girl. We fill ourselves with something we think is right and good for ourselves. What we choose has different effects on our lives. We are always doing our best, every time, always. Our capabilities and abilities are just different every step of the way.

I was disconnected from myself, and it did not matter what I put into my life. I had nothing to compare it to because I did not know what to compare it to. I was lost. I borrowed other people's judgments because mine were lost. I didn't know how to feel because I did not feel myself. I kept going and going, trying this and that. Some things worked. Others did not, did not give me the love and kindness that I was looking for. Did not feed my heart's needs. Then one day, I realized that I was looking for myself because the other things did not work and gave me nothing because I was nothing without myself.

I was looking for myself, looking for a place I belonged to because I did not belong with me. My subconscious mind kept me going, and I did not know that. I was lost, searching for myself. My subconscious mind sent me here and there. I found a place and matured and grew there a little bit. When I could not develop more there, it sent me somewhere else. Little by little, I evolved and grew more and found myself, piece by piece. I realized that every place, every person, and every life has meaning. We are constantly giving each other gifts of maturity, developing each other, and becoming better than yesterday. Sometimes the gifts are a little bit strange, the packaging complex, they hurt you, cut you, almost break you because of their weight, but they always have a purpose. A new vision, depth, growth, and life are more extensive than yesterday. My glass is always full for the rest of my life. This morning, during lunch, all day. Tonight, I will fall asleep and cannot drink more. I am alive. I have drained yesterday's cup, which will never fill up again. But tomorrow I will get a new full glass. In fact, the only option I have is to enjoy the rest of my life—one day at a time.

My memories were hidden for almost 40 years. I was living with the consequences of the sexual abuse that I endured as a child from men outside of my family. My life was not functioning, and I was endlessly running into hidden walls in my daily life. I asked my Higher Power, as I understood it, why it was hidden for such a long time. I did not get the answer immediately, but it came to me eventually. Here it is:

The child within me must be able to trust me, in the Now, to handle its problems. It needs to see and trust that I can handle what is buried within. That I can resolve what happened to it, walk it through the pain, and set it free. I know that it loves me and has protected me all these years, knowing that I would not handle its story without the mental tools that I have today. Otherwise, it would have told me what happened to it a long time ago. I will do my best to be capable of dealing with its story and set it free from the pain. I will show it the same love as it has shown me. There is a solution to everything.

WHERE DOES THE PAIN COME FROM?

The big questions regarding our pain within and this strange state of our minds are: How did this enormous pain emerge inside us? What is actually going on, and what can I do about it?

These are big questions, and I think that nobody knows them entirely, but I have a theory, and I hope it will help you to understand what is going on. Here is what I believe is the cause and effect, the process towards a peaceful and fulfilling life.

The coping mechanism is not a treatment. It is a survival state. Like any bodily wound and the pain that follows, the wounds and pain of the mind and emotions also need to be treated and healed. The simple answer is if there is still pain, then the wound has not healed yet, and the completion of Breaking Free has not been accomplished.

I hope that this will help you to gain an understanding of your situation and the clarity to address your state of

74 Working Towards Equilibrium After Trauma

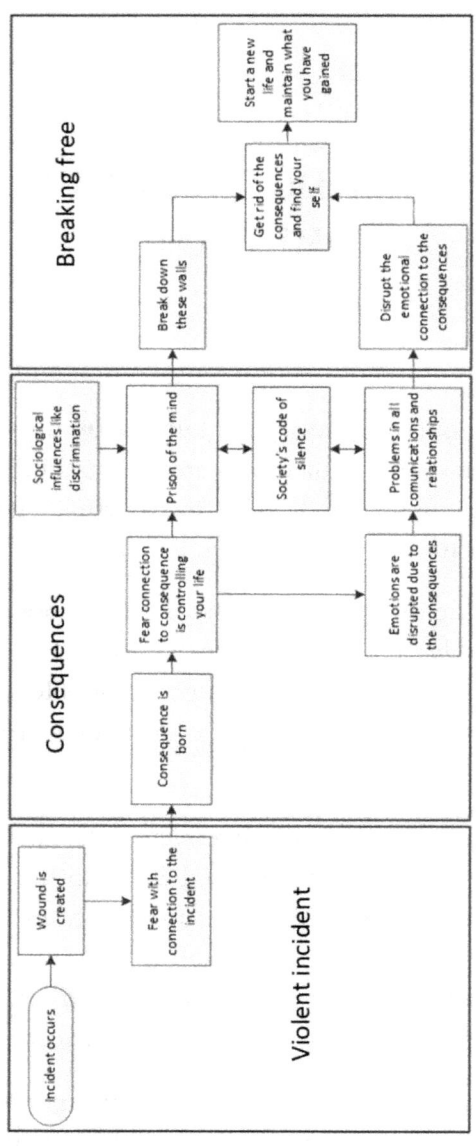

Figure 6: The Big Picture

mind in a manner that brings you peace of mind. I also like to pass on understanding and clarity to the ones who have a person in their lives who is suffering from something intangible hidden in their past.

Here is the big picture as I see it.

Let's break it down and dig into how I understand it:

Violent Incident

A violent act that was performed on us can be tangible and/or intangible. Have in mind that there does not need to be broken bones and blood for there to be a violent act taking place.

Tangible physical actions can inflict varying degrees of bodily harm and leave marks or wounds on our bodies. A tangible act will always create an intangible wound in our inner being. How much and how deep does not matter; there are always consequences for any action.

In the cases where there is not an infliction of a bodily wound but a violent act to our core being, there is always an intangible wound created in our inner being. How much and how deep? It does not matter.

These violent acts can be hidden in plain sight. They can be part of a culture, part of communication patterns in families, companies, sports, a fellowship of any kind, and many more.

Getting exposed to gaslighting, when an opinion of somebody towards you is that everything you do is wrong or never enough, is an example of an intangible violent act towards your mind and emotions.

When you are talking down to yourself it is also a violent act. When we are trying to control others for their own good, then we are in violation of their freedom. At the same time, we are constantly disappointed with ourselves because of our failure to accomplish control over others. Nobody can or should control others. It is a violent act, and it will always fail. It will lead to a prescription for failure against ourselves. Violence is violence, no matter how it is performed.

So, let's walk through the boxes.

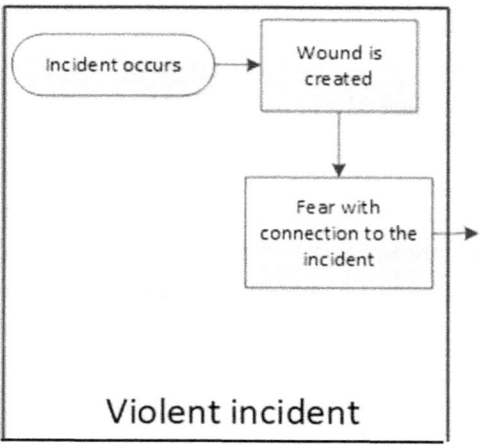

Figure 7: Violent Incident

Incident Occurs

There is a violent act toward someone. It does not matter if it leaves behind a bodily wound or not. There is always a wound, though you cannot see it visually.

Wounds Are Created

There are always wounds, and nothing is too small. Bodily wounds are simple to see, but the wounds that manifest in the inner being are hidden. If you have a bodily wound, then you will also have wounds in your inner being.

The Fear in Connection to the Incident

Fear starts to manifest within you related to the incident. It can be fear of the location of the incident, the smell, the colors, what was in the surroundings, the date of it, the time of it, the gender of the violator, the connection to the violator, the age, character traits, the motive of your meeting that individual, and more.

Consequences

Consequences of abuse are one of the most hidden issues of our time, and probably have been for centuries, and some of them are accepted as the right way of communicating with others. It was hidden from me for decades. I was clueless about it until after breaking free from it all.

The most important way to stop us from entering the spiral of consequential behavior is for somebody to step in when we are in the first box, when Consequence is born, and tell us that what happened was not our fault. To lay down all the facts about the incident and convince us that we carry no responsibility for it all. To go to the police or any other fitting institute, and at least speak out, not bury everything inside, which would only lead to self-blaming and destruction. The shorter time we stay in this box, the better! If you know somebody who is there, by all means, step in!

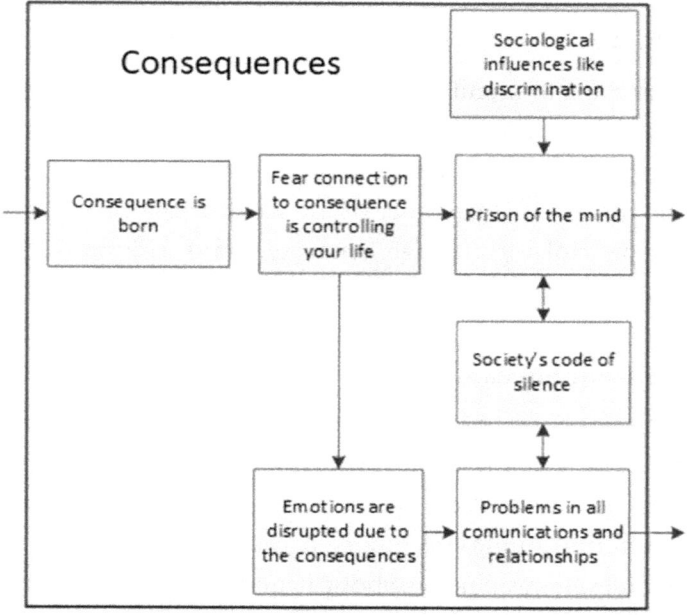

Figure 8: Consequences

The consequences were all over my life, in all areas. If I had to say what they did not affect, I would state my name and stay silent, with nothing more to say.

What is crucial about this stage of the process is the time spent there. The longer time one spends there, the more effect it will have, and the longer time it takes to break free from it. It is like a spiral. In the beginning, we are at the edge of entering the vortex. It is starting to pull us in, and if we do not stop, we get drawn in, and little by little, we lose control over our lives according to how close we are to the center of the spiral.

Let us walk through the boxes.

Consequence Is Born

At this point, a short time has passed since the incident. The dust is settling, and the reality of it all begins to sink in. The trauma gives birth to the consequences, which start to take shape, unfolding in the following processes.

Fear Connection to the Consequences Is Controlling Our Life

Here, the fear manifests in our minds and emotions related to the incident. You can become afraid of the location of the incident, the smell, the colors, what was in the surroundings, the date of it, the time of it, the gender of the violator, the connection to the violator, the character, the age, the scenario of your meeting that individual, everything related to the incident.

Prison of the Mind

We start to build mental and emotional walls around us for our protection. Brick by brick, we build up protective walls around us. If we stay in this state for a long time, then these walls will turn into a prison.

Emotions Are Disrupted Due to the Consequences

You start to have emotional reactions towards everyone and everything. Nothing is excluded! Consequential behavior or reactions are your first response to everything and everybody.

Problems in All Communications and Relationships

We have no idea how emotions, in general, work. We have lost the ability to read emotional signals in front of us when communicating with others and have also lost control in processing emotions within as well as conveying our emotional responses to others. In short, it is a total mess.

Sociological Influences such as Discrimination

We often stand out in many ways. We can be dysfunctional in communications, and the ways we numb ourselves from the pain are not always socially accepted. When we do not fit into the norm, we can be discriminated against as a result.

Society's Code of Silence

Secrets are, in all cases, a problem. Communication with anybody who is trying to keep a secret will be obscured, and dishonesty will be in the air. It is never good, never! They say that the truth cannot withstand the light, but it is the darkness that comes up to the surface following the truth that people have problems handling. We have to gain the ability to handle the darkness.

Break Free

How deeply and how fast each is capable of working on their issues is up to the individual, not others. If we go too fast and get ahead of ourselves, it can be harmful, even dangerous. Pushing somebody through the process is not the right way to go about it. If you want to push somebody through the process, you must ask yourself, are you doing it for yourself or the person in pain? It is crucial for our loved ones to let go and be there and reflect in an honest and loving manner on us who are in the process of breaking free. We are not afraid to die. We are afraid to live. We do not know how to live, but we are on our way.

If you find yourself in a situation where you think that everybody is better off without you—that if you take your life, everyone will be better off—that state of mind is a clear indication that you have gotten ahead of yourself in digging into your wounds. So, if that state of mind occurs, you need to slow down and look at your accomplishments so far and nurture yourself until that state subsides.

Nobody is better off without you. On the contrary, it can be that you are in the wrong company with people who are not right for you. I hope that the content here will help you stand up from that state of mind. Remember that the thought of taking your life is a hoax, not a reality! Though the idea seems so real that it feels like it is tangible, it is not! It is a byproduct of the consequences, and you are in the midst of the spiral—but it will be okay. I have been there numerous times, I know! Once, I argued with this voice for over three hours during a drive out in the country; it felt so real, but it was not. I am here. If I can be here, then you can also!

If you are in the company of individuals who are urging you to leave us for good, leave *them* for good! We love you! I am here! You are here! It will be okay!

So, let us walk through the boxes.

Breaking Down These Walls

To break down a wall, you have to see the wall. If we do not realize what is bothering our inner being, then we have nothing to work with or work on, and we do not see the walls all around us, our prison. We have isolated ourselves from the world. We have built walls so that nobody could get to us and hurt us again.

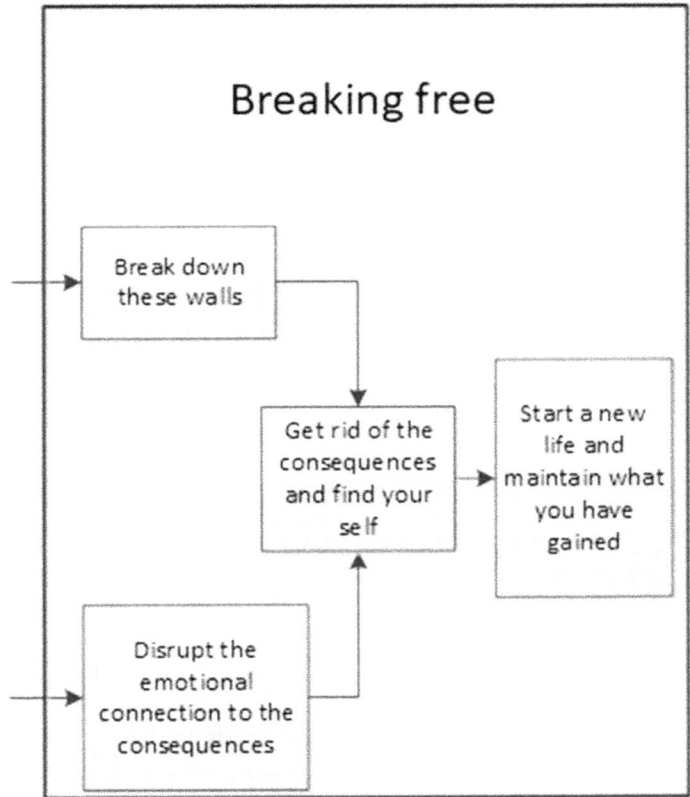

Figure 9: Breaking Free

Disrupt the Emotional Connection to the Consequences

It is pretty simple; all of our emotional life is diluted by the consequences of the trauma we endured. Our inner life is full of consequences leading us to be in the form of a mental coma state. Nobody died! There is learned behavior in our response to everything. Are our reactions defensive reactions? Or are they loving and kind? Are we in fight, flight, or freeze responses when something triggers us? We must dig into our reflections on our daily life and figure out our reactions to situations throughout the day when we interact with others. Find the patterns and disrupt them. Find the red flag, grab it, and gain control over it. Since this is a learned behavior, that means that we can learn to respond differently.

Get Rid of the Consequences and Find Yourself

We must break free from the consequential behavior and find our true inner being that has been kept down by the consequences. Find a solution that fits you. Though you have been running into invisible walls so far, it does not mean that your answer is not out there; it simply means that you have not found it yet. Go through these books and the blog and pick up what suits your need and build on that. There is no one answer that fits everybody. Keep on looking and assemble your toolbox. All that matters is your mental and emotional toolbox. After all, it is your life. You have to find your true self, and nobody else can do that for you. You are full of strength and wisdom that you have accumulated throughout your lifespan. That is your foundation. You are here, aren't you? That means that you are a solutionoriented being and a seeker. If I can, so can you!

Start a New Life and Maintain What We Have Gained

We have worked through our issues and found our true authentic selves. This can be the tricky part. We know constant pain and conflicts in all aspects of our lives. Now there is peace, and we have no idea how to deal with that. We are standing with our true authentic selves, our true emotional state, and we do not know how to apply it in our life. We have to be careful, so we do not fall into our old patterns. "One step at a time" has a new meaning. We need to examine all aspects of our life and discover what it is we truly desire in each facet of our life. It is in no way a bad place to be in. It is a great place to be at but, at the same time, very complicated. The good news is that we get to choose what we put into our lives. It is trial and error in many ways, and that is okay. It is your life, and you are in charge! What do you want to do with your life? What do you need to maintain your freedom and continue to grow and mature as the beautiful soul that you are?

Go out there and start building something beautiful! Follow your heart! It knows the way!

FORGIVENESS—WHAT IS IT?

Sometimes language and culture can be a barrier. Word meanings and traditions that are very strongly associated with a particular culture and with a particular language can disrupt healing. Certain words can look and feel all twisted up and out of proportion.

Our beautiful Icelandic language is no exception to that. It can be confusing at times, mixing this and that with the consequences of the other, resulting in us not taking some steps that are beneficial to us.

Forgiveness is one of these words. We are, in most cases, raised in the manner that "Forgiveness" involves other meanings that are irrelevant to it, like "to make peace" with the other party. When I was growing up and a conflict came up, not necessarily my fault, we had to shake hands and both say "Sorry" and go back to playing.

So, if we accumulate the actions that occurred:

> I had to say "sorry"—though I had done nothing wrong.
>
> I had to forgive—though I was not ready for it at that moment.
>
> I had to make peace with that person—though it was against my will.
>
> I had to let that person in again—with the risk of his harming me again.
>
> I had to trust—though I was not ready at that moment nor ever will be.

This happened all at once, combined into a single action. It was a completely useless learning experience, and it got in the way of progressing my life from that moment. I was angry and frustrated at some people, and with this learning experience, I was stuck to that person. I am letting somebody live in my head rent-free, and I do not even like that person. I hated him! At the same time, I was not in the present moment in my life; it was crowded in my head, and everybody was fighting. We must be careful of what we teach our children.

If you think about it, all these actions have nothing to do with the matter at hand! To forgive does not mean that person is reconciled with, approved of, trusted, and brought back into your life or anything in that manner.

The implementation of Forgiving is in fact a detachment, letting go of something or someone, nothing more, nothing less.

That I forgive (let go) means that I am no longer thinking about the person—I get freedom from that person. Therefore, I can be thinking about something else, and the feeling about that person does not control me anymore. I am not taking anyone back into my life, trusting again, or anything in that way. I will get rid of that person if I chose to do so. I am free!

Forgiveness is Forgiveness. In practice, it is letting go, nothing more. I am in charge of whom I trust, make peace with, let back into my life, and it is my choice.

I have learned that when I let go of somebody or something, I become happier.

THE MYTH OF VICTIMS BECOMING ABUSERS

There is no direct connection between being a victim of abuse and perpetuating this abuse themselves. I do not know how many people I have talked out of suicide just because of this myth which caused the individuals to become so afraid of harming others, of becoming monsters themselves. We must put this myth to rest.

VOCABULARY ABOUT SEXUAL ABUSE

Let us be perfectly clear. An individual of any gender is in no way responsible for being a victim of sexual abuse. It does not matter if the individual in question is at home or outside, sober or non-sober, dressed or naked. Nobody asks for being sexually abused! Nothing justifies a violent act of any kind! Everybody has the possibility of walking away from initiating a violent action.

We need to discuss these issues responsibly. We need to talk to everyone, to all genders. We need to take care of how we speak about it since it happens to all genders, and the perpetrators can be both women and men, all genders. If we say that only children and women are victims, then the message is that if you are a man, it could not have happened to you, that men are not abused, only children and women are.

If we only talk about men as perpetrators, we are doing two things. First, we are telling women and men that are victims of violence performed by women that it did not happen. Women do not do these things. Second, we are telling women abusers that they did not and are not doing anything wrong. Only men do these things. The responsibility is being taken away from them. Women abused by women are in an especially dangerous place since the discussion about female abusers is too hidden. It is almost entirely off the table. There is almost nothing in society that admits that it could have happened to them. Research shows that the abuser's gender does not matter regarding consequences for the abused.

If you decide to press charges for the violence that you lived through, then you are in no way responsible for the upcoming uproar that follows the exposure. The abuser is responsible, not you!

Discussion is a good thing. It brings these issues out into the light, which needs to happen. Too many people decide to end their lives every year—children, women, and men. There is only one way to destroy the darkness, and that is to shine a loving light on it and bring it out into the open.

Education given with kindness and love will always bring success. We are all brothers and sisters, and together we can accomplish everything. It is the drop that hollows out the stone, and many drops together can achieve incredible things.

IT IS OFTEN SAID THAT THE TRUTH CANNOT STAND THE LIGHT.

Actually, it is the ugliness that comes with the truth that people have problems with. Truth can always stand the light.

We, the Homo Sapiens, tend to be defensive. Probably because we want things to be nice, say nice things, and pretend our life is admirable. We are creatures too busy maintaining an image, keeping things smooth on the surface, and saying everything is good in our lives. Most people tend to look at each other and say: "Oh, how I would like to have that life; it looks fantastic." At least we want others to look at us and think that way. The need for recognition is strong in us.

But what is the reality? A stage play where everything needs to be kept in line and nothing is wrong; you cannot say this and that. All because somebody might have an opinion about it. Is this living? No, I do not think so.

People fight to keep the ugliness in the darkness, mainly because this species does not know what to do with it. It does not fit the ideal image.

The truth guided by love and kindness will always win in the end. It is the ugliness that wants to stay in the dark. Let us shine the light of love and kindness on the ugliness; the ugliness will not be able to survive it. Ugliness will be driven away and leave only the timeless truth, with love and kindness left standing shining on the one who needs it the most, the victim.

We have to gain the ability to handle the ugliness and face the big picture. I believe that some people's reactions to the ugliness might have something to do with their own pain within that they have not dealt with, their own wounds that they do not have the ability to handle.

The gifts of life will often arrive in strange packages. It will sometimes take a very long time to figure out the package and how to unfold it. Still, the wonderful thing about this life is that there is always a gift behind everything, something that matters to you today and tomorrow, not yesterday. Yesterday is gone, and it does not matter because yesterday is over. Today is what matters. It is a gift. That is why it's called a present.

MY MENTAL DIRT PIT

Life happens. We are constantly invited to mental parties by others. Some parties are great, but others are not so great. My ability to select the parties that I am invited to differs from day to day. Sometimes my center is not in my true center, which can put me in a vulnerable position, and I end up in a mental party that is not in my best interest.

Here is an example of me in a mental party that was not in my best interest, not in my center, and I lost the grip of my responses in my life due to the ingredients of the party. I fell into my consequential responses and went on a journey into my darkness. The good news about that journey is that when I stand up again and have taken the wisdom from it, I am stronger, having gained understanding and knowledge of what triggered me. There is less danger of my falling again under the same circumstances that I was facing.

If we look at the graph then for the first 9 days of the month, I am above my consequential responses in my daily life. Life is normal. My emotional responses are in the love and kindness spectrum; there is peace in my life.

On day 10, I am in front of a situation that triggers my wounds, and they kind of escape from the lovingkindness spectrum and go back into my defensive spectrum. I have entered the defensive response, fight, flight, or freeze. My trauma wounds have opened up because there was a situation that I had not dealt with before. Everything opens up, and I am back into the pain. My self-esteem falls, and the pain is everywhere. I grab my tool chest and immediately start to work on this pain that has emerged. I try to identify the source and what is causing this all. On day 17, I finally figure out what was causing all this. I have found the wound, cleaned it, healed it, nourished it, and understood what caused it all. My selfesteem has started to rise again, I have gained a new understanding, and I am stronger than ever before. Life is good again, much better than before. I am out of my mental dirt pit.

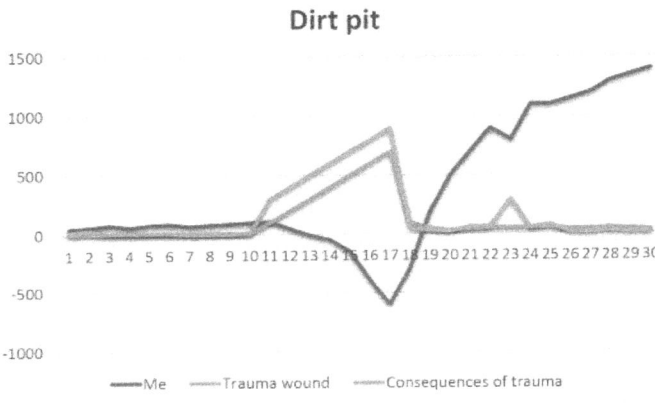

Figure 10: Dirt Pit

INTERNAL PAIN IS GOOD IN ITS OWN NATURE.

It tells us what is wrong inside. The Pain is the lead that takes us to the source, what we need to work on to get a better life. It is the mirror image of our soul for what needs to be healed. It does not define you. It is only the state you are in at each given moment. Grab it with loving arms, not with fear. Tell it that it will be okay. You in the now, and your inner being at the time when the wound was created will figure it out together.

I cannot turn off The Pain. I have to *process* it!

I DID NOT DIE – I WENT INTO A COMA STATE – I CAN GET BACK!

There is a big misconception about our affairs. There are so many who say that we died. They could not be more wrong. We did not die. We went into a coma state—a mental and emotional coma state. We are at the ICU, and we are waiting and searching for the right tools to treat this coma state. Nothing more. We are alive, but there is a certain dysfunction in our life. We are in a fight, flight, or freeze state. That is totally different. People talk about us like we are dead and can be treated like that. Some are even afraid of touching us. We are of no use in this society as human beings. We are not sustainable in our life, and we should be taken care of in accordance with that. We do not have a chance anymore in this lifetime. Too common a statement is that we *are* our consequential behavior. It cannot be further from the truth. That treatment is a violent act toward us. It is discrimination, and we need to change that. Not only do we need to educate ourselves, but we have to educate our society, family members, friends, and the caretakers who are supposed to be the specialists on our issues. We are in this together, and together we can make everybody's life better.

Nobody died. We are here, though our emotional and mental state is in a coma. I was there. I was in an emotional and mental coma. If it were a relationship status, then it would say, "It is complicated." I found the tools that suited my state of mind and emotional being. If I could do it, you can. I believe in you!

JUST ANGER OR JUSTIFIABLE ANGER

There is a difference between those two, but they are both dangerous. I know that both states of mind will hurt me if I am out of control in them.

Justified anger is usually a response in the now to someone who is treating me badly. Normal response to justified anger does not last long if I respond properly in most cases. When someone oversteps my boundaries, I always respond and express myself in retrospect to the love and respect for myself and my life at each moment in time. My goal is always to react according to the adversity but not with violence. If I have expressed myself and set boundaries accordingly, the anger goes away. If I do not express myself or go overboard, then the event will stay with me until I have expressed myself in equilibrium to my inner being and to the adversity. Have in mind that when we are rejecting a behavior, we are not rejecting the person.

Justifiable anger does not sound too good. It feels to me like someone will take up the right to be angry. That someone will take an event from the past and light a fire with it inside to reach a very bad place within himself or herself. Then that person will justify the situation because of something which usually has nothing to do with the present. That is a dangerous situation which is difficult to justify. Somebody will get hurt! I will do my very best to not go there! There are better ways to deal with the past than this.

By reviewing my responses, I can learn more about myself and work on issues that I am not happy with. You know it in your heart. Are you still in a turbulent state or are you at peace?

The key issue is that carrying anger for the long run will always hurt the one who is carrying it the most. At the same time, it is a normal feeling, and it takes time to master.

It is up to us to do something about it; after all, it is our life.

CATEGORIZING FEAR

I have learned that my life has been over-controlled by fear most of my life.

Fear itself is a learned behavior from when we were walking through life and were faced with a dangerous situation. Throughout our lifespan, we face all kinds of situations, and we categorize these situations in our brain as safe or unsafe. This is an excellent system for us to get out of or not go into harmful situations, kind of a baseline for our lives and our surroundings. In Iceland, nature itself can be as dangerous as its beauty is. The hot lava flow is spectacular, but we do not go river rafting in it. So, the baseline for traveling in Iceland is—never go river rafting in a hot lava river.

Another example: If somebody had been kind and loving to us and then violated us after being kind and loving, then we put kindness and loving into the danger category. We also might put that person's smell, characteristics, color, the color of their clothes and ours, everything related to the incident that occurred that caused our trauma into the danger category. That becomes the root of our traumatic responses related to this incident. By repeating these traumatic responses through our journey through life, we start to put bricks around us to protect ourselves from these dangerous situations. With each interaction and use of these responses, we add another brick to this protective wall, layer by layer, and in the end, it will become our prison. Have you ever wondered why you get into conflict with other people?

When we face our fear, we talk to it, embrace it, and listen to it. I tell the fear that I will listen to what it has to say, that I will not run away from it anymore, that we will figure out together what is going on. It will be okay; it does not have to run my life anymore. Then the fear subsides and eases the grip that it has on our life because we are listening to what it has to say. By doing that, one step at a time, one day at a time, we start to recategorize the way we define what should be in the danger zone and what should not. Then we begin to take down the walls of our prison, one brick at a time.

It will be okay. If I could do it, so can you.

THE SHAKING OF COCA-COLA® SYNDROME

We tend to sit on our emotions and feelings, and we do everything we can to keep a lid on them. Behind these emotions and feelings are often secrets that we feel that we are the reason for bad things that happened in our life. We will take these secrets with us to the grave, but actually, they are taking us to the grave. By the way, it is not your fault that a person did some bad things to you. Never! It is *that* person's fault.

We sit on our feelings and emotions because we lack the ability to handle them and have no idea what to do with them and how they work. By sitting on them, then we are waiting, unaware, for an eruption. One day they will blow up in our faces. It is like a ticking time bomb.

When we start to open up these hidden feelings and emotions, they tend to be overwhelming in the beginning. They will overflow. It is much like you taking a Coca-Cola bottle, shaking it well, then opening it up immediately, and the soda will burst up into the air like a geyser and spill over everything in its vicinity. It is okay; let it flow. It is inevitable. It will subside, and equilibrium will be reached. You can look at the big picture of the overflow and try to see the cognitive stage of its being. It can help you to find the age that you were when the trauma was taking place.

When that happens, we need to be kind to the situation and ourselves. We kept a lid on them because we had no ability or tools to deal with them before. We have to let them flow and gain equilibrium. It can look like a nervous breakdown, but it is okay. Do not try to make sense of it but try to make sense of why you got there.

It is like the North American and Eurasian tectonic plates at Lake Thingvellir here in Iceland during the Ice Age. Nowadays, the tectonic plates move apart about 2 to 4 cm each year, but during the Ice Age, the movement on the surface was kept in the grip of the ice, and underneath, there was a tension buildup. When the Ice Age lifted, the ice let go of its grip on the surface, and the builtup tension underneath got released. That resulted in a vast movement on the surface. The tectonic plates moved apart rapidly, and the area in between plummeted down. The same thing happens to our feelings and emotions. If there is an obstacle to expressing them, they get built up. When we let them out, there can be an outburst. The end result of the vast movement of the tectonic plates is the phenomenal, extremely beautiful valley and Lake Thingvellir that we admire every day. The same thing will apply to our life when the soda eruption subsides; a beautiful, emotional feeling connected to that particular emotion that was submerged will arise.

These were catastrophic events, both of them. It is not easy to be in the vicinity during the release of the tension, which will affect all of our surrounding areas. The end result is beautiful in both cases when equilibrium is reached. Totally worth it.

I LOVE MY SO-CALLED FLAWS.

Without them, I would have died as a child.

They saved my life so many times. If I had not developed defensive reflexes to disconnect me from the pain at that time in my life, I would not have survived. Nothing in my environment told me that what was happening was wrong and was not my fault. Nobody stepped in and stopped what was going on. Nobody came running and took me out of this hostile environment. There is only one way to survive, and that is to develop and master mental techniques to protect myself in circumstances that I could not have control over. These cognitive techniques are called fight, flight, or freeze. In my case, it was part of the flight responses—freezing numbness. I fled into myself, disconnecting me from the world, and it helped me get through life until I got into a solution-based environment that I knew I could trust, where I gained the ability to take on things connected to the pain inside of me. A safe environment where I knew that it was okay to open the memory bank.

Though I had entered the solutionbased environment and learned new techniques, it was tough to let go of these old survival techniques. They were so strong and so intertwined in my being, always wanting to step in and take over, to save me even though I did not need to be saved. They were everywhere, in all aspects of my life.

I need to treat those socalled flaws with respect, love, and care. I need them to know that it is all right. We are no longer alone in our defense mechanism, barely surviving. We do not need to react like that anymore. We are safe. It is okay to let go.

It takes time to disconnect the old techniques and let new ones take over. It is all right; time will pass no matter what. I respect the old techniques, and I am grateful for them since they saved my life.

WRIGHT BROTHERS SYNDROME

When we are reflecting on the past, we have to be careful not to fall into guilt traps towards ourselves. We cannot apply today's knowledge and understanding of life to incidents that were in the past regarding our responses to them. If we do that, then we are being violent towards ourselves. At every given moment in our life, we were honest to the best of our ability, and we have to treat ourselves in that manner. We did our best each time.

The only thing we can do is to apply today's knowledge and understanding to these occasions, learn from them, and do better in the future. Then we have turned those incidents into a gift; we have become stronger.

If we are still stuck in the statement "I should have done better" and insist that today's knowledge and understanding applies to the past, we can say that this statement is true: "The Wright brothers should have used a turbofan engine in their first flight in 1903." This statement does not hold water, nor should I have done better in the past. Let go, take the lesson, and make the future better. Rearview mirrors are facing backward, and we are not going there.

PRESENT DEFENSE REFLEXES AND THEIR RESISTANCE TO CHANGE

I realize that my emotional reflexes that have caused me anger and disappointment today are the result of the past and have nothing to do with the reality of today.

Your old defense reflexes that are operating within you in the present will resist these changes, and that is all right. Your inner being will need to learn to trust the process, and it will.

These reflexes were connected to the consequences of the things I went through and do not necessarily represent real anger and disappointment. The anger and disappointment are great indicators of my mental state and are telling me what I need to be working on regarding my issues. I welcome them as guidelines on what I need to work on and be strong at. I will take an honest look at myself and use my strengths to help me get through this process. I know that my dear friend, my Higher Power, will be by my side, and without my Higher Power, I cannot do this.

THE INFRASTRUCTURE WE BUILD INSIDE

During the time we have spent in a fight, flight, or freeze state, we build up an infrastructure, a mechanism that we structure our survivalism on. After we get out of our fight, flight, or freeze state and consequential behavior patterns and into our freedom, we will have the infrastructure without the emotional turmoil. That is a tool that will benefit us for the rest of our life. What your behavior pattern is will come to you. Only you know. It is different for different people. But it is there, and it will emerge. I do not know when, but if you keep on working on all the issues that arise, then it will come to you one day. For me, it was excellent project management skills. I was always helping everybody with everything, without their asking me. I was the nice guy whom everybody called. In reality, I was having an impact in a smooth and nice way on everything around me so I could cope with what was happening and what was ahead in my life.

That left me with strong skills in organizing, planning, managing, and executing many things at the same time. A good friend and colleague told me that if I were not such an excellent project manager then I would never have pulled off the publishing of the book *Ferðalag til frelsis* ("Journey to Freedom") in Icelandic. In fact, I can thank my infrastructure for this recovery program coming to life. I am very happy about that!

WHAT IS FAITH? WHO OR WHAT IS MY HIGHER POWER?

I think that all of us have faith differing only in what we choose to believe in. Everyone has his or her beliefs, which is the only way to go. The big issue on this journey is that we need to be connected to something higher than ourselves that we can trust and that gives us love, something to which we can give our secrets to. Something that is in direct connection with our inner being, always, every day. There is no person who can fulfill this role for us, just our version of Higher Power. If you are against it, try finding yours just while going through this process, and you can always return it when you are done.

It is good to choose a name that does not have a connection with fear and/or submission. This is just our choice, and you choose yours. My Higher Power is a divine energy, above religions. It is the light and love of the universe that shines and embraces everything with love and kindness. Religion, for me, is more like a lifestyle. Where we are regarding religion has more to do with where we were born and what religion governs our society. There is no religion that is higher than others. We are all equal. We are all awesome!

I believe that there is something higher than us. Something that is more than us. Something that is kind of the baseline for our emotional life, that is the theme of how we react to stimuli that comes to us. It is always a choice, and we have free will. Are our reactions to life positive or negative? Is our Higher Power a punishing being or approaching us in a kind and loving manner as a caring being? Is it leading us to shame or a learning curve? How do we react to a traffic light on our way home during rush hour? Calmly or with impatience? Is a person we are thinking about constantly overtaking our mind—in fact, our life? What about when the car we're driving breaks down? Do we accept it as part of life or feel annoyed and frustrated? Am I punishing myself, or am I learning? How do I react to things that come into my life and push my emotions? What is the core base of my Higher Power? The choice is mine; I have free will.

We all are constantly reacting according to our belief system and the way we understand it. Our understanding is our way. Our understanding is always the right one for us. We have an emotional relationship with what we believe in, according to how we understand it. Anything else is not right for us. It is right for someone else but not us. So basically, we have our free will and our Higher Power.

Regarding our world as a victim of violence, there is an added complexity. There was an incident, one or more, injected into our life without our approval. Each incident leaves a mark inside of us, and that mark follows us and can govern us in a negative manner until we heal what is left within us and the consequences of it go away. That can influence us so strongly that these negative marks start to be the leading influencer in our internal functional mechanism. That function is the fight, flight, or freeze response that we go into to survive each day in our lives until healing takes place. So, our fight, flight, or freeze system becomes our second belief system, and in a way, it will become our second Higher Power.

So, to sum up, we have our free will, our fight, flight, or freeze system, and our Higher Power—a fairly complex system that leads to chaos. It will be okay; you are on your way to unwind the complexity into clarity.

OPERATIONAL PRACTICES

My biggest strength is also my biggest weakness, and vice versa. If I have patience and kindness, I am operating in the mode that my positive Higher Power guides me in, and there is love and kindness in that. If I have stubbornness and inflexibility, I am operating in either my fight, flight, or freeze responses or the negative Higher Power mode, and there is darkness—a bad place to be in.

We are always operating our life each day but with a varied approach. We are always doing our best. It is up to us what we want to have, and the result is based on our ability to achieve it. On which side is our life better? We need to gain the ability to choose and clarity to see the big picture.

WHERE DO YOU WANT TO GO?

The state of our soul. Where are we at any given state of our being?

What really is the state of our soul, the way our mind works? How is it possible to put the mindset into perspective in the case of victims of sexual violence, the way of thinking, compared to what we call the "normal" way of thinking? One way of explaining it is by using Abraham Maslow's hierarchy of needs. I disagree with him though about the highest level, called *self-actualization*. His theory states that very few of us reach that level. I think all of us are there, all day, every day, standing on our own platform of personal growth and cognitive abilities at each given moment. That is the Present, in all its glory, the Now. The quality of the Present is determined by one's foundation of growth, cognitive stage, and some more of what we have accumulated until now. It does not change the fact that we are always in our own Present, our own Now. All I can do is to try to improve it to the best of my ability, one step at a time, one day at a time.

What controls the things happening in the Present at each point in time? Do we realize what is really going on? Do we have the tools to look at ourselves and change if we are unhappy with what we see? If we do not have the tools necessary, then there is only one thing to do. Find the right tools that fit you and your life. That is the only thing we need to do to improve ourselves. First of all, we need to gain an understanding of what is going on in our lives. The following is one way to do that.

The Foundation

The picture below shows what are considered the normal aspects of being human, i.e., what is needed, what comes first, and what the essential elements are. One thing that determines our behavior is our need to be acknowledged. It greatly determines how we treat ourselves and others. Where do we feed our self-esteem? If it is in the right place, everything is balanced, but if placed in the wrong order, things start to go wrong.

The Optimal Situation

Let's imagine we are like the tree in the picture. We are out and about in life, and everything is going our way. The branches are our feelings, and the leaves are our emotional experiences. The wind is the circumstances in our life, what is going on, and the mental parties that we are invited to enter.

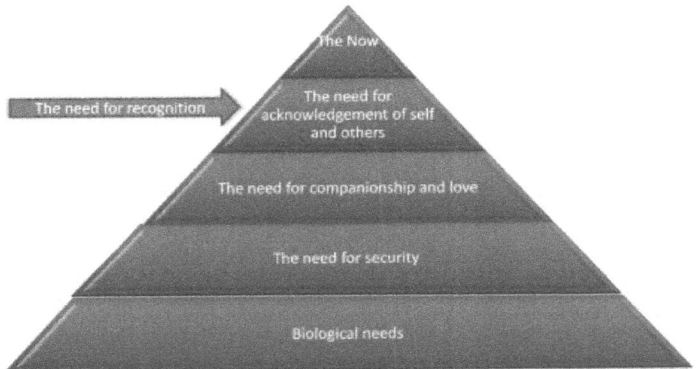

Figure 11: The Optimal Now

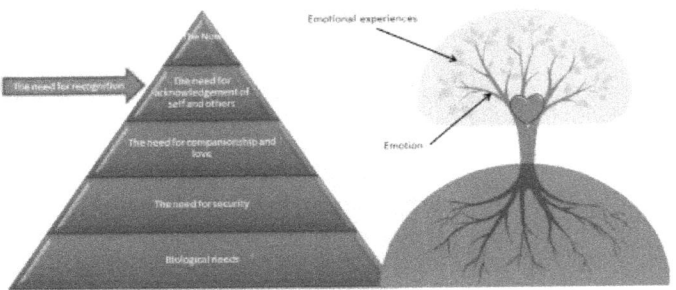

Figure 12: Theory Merged into Life

What Does It Mean?

When everything is going well, the wind blows through the leaves, the sun warms us, the rain waters us, the tree trunk protects us from injuries, the roots are fed correctly, and we experience life in a comfortable and happy way.

The need for being acknowledged is placed correctly, and the tree is doing fine. Nothing is going to tilt us over because emotional responses following the wind are based on solid ground and hierarchy and are not controlled by survival consequential behavior related to our trauma.

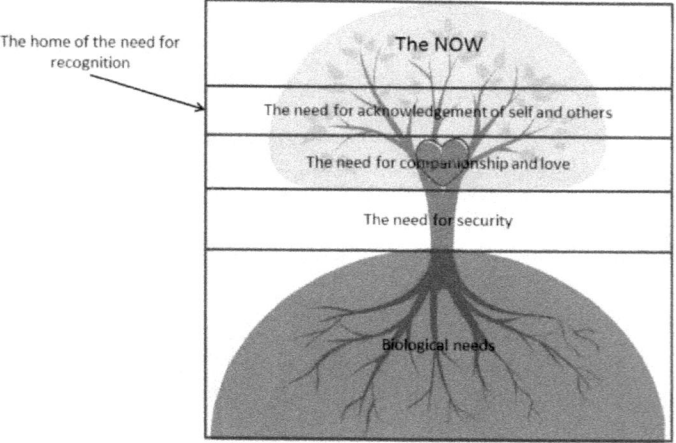

Figure 13: Healthy Life

If these things are balanced, our expectations are in the right place, which means that disappointment is not a significant factor in our life. The Present (the Now) is good, and life is going our way. All our needs are met, and we stand firm in our life.

The Reality for Victims of Violence

We have the tendency to hang on to one emotion, often related to our trauma. That emotion can be anger, love, or the need for love, and at the same time, the need for acknowledgment, the feeling of justice, joy, food, or something else. In these instances, we stand on one emotion in life. Our total emotional existence is built upon it. We crave acknowledgment through that one emotion, and our entire life is focused on it. We start behaving in line with those needs. We do not allow ourselves the right to live, and we start to justify our life from and through this emotion. All the things we value are centered on it. Extreme behavior is aimed at satisfying it, and we tend to go further and further in this direction. Behavior, sometimes called addiction, comes from this focus. The truth of the matter is that we are just trying to survive. We are actually solutionoriented and have found a way to channel our pain out of the darkness into something that seems to be working; at least with a break from the pain, temporarily, we are alive.

The need for acknowledgment/recognition is placed in the wrong place. We will do everything to be acknowledged and recognized as a person who deserves to be alive. To exist. To be included. We do not have personal freedom.

Emotional integrity is built upon our needs and, at the same time, our entire existence. When something happens that rocks our emotional reason for living, a

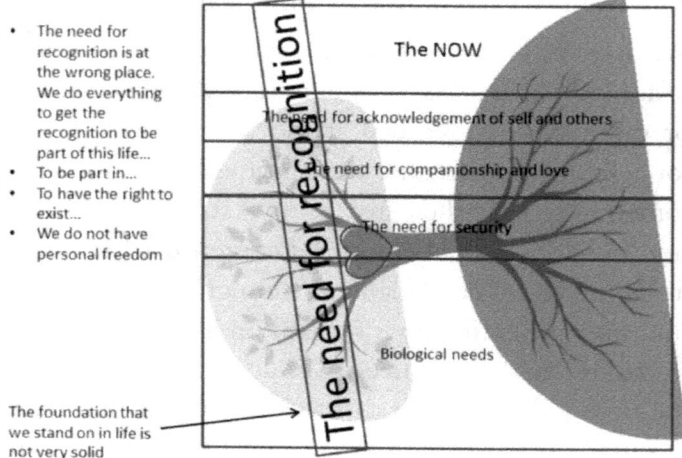

Figure 14: The Need for Recognition
Is Controlling Our Lives

dangerous situation arises for us. We often fight back because the event endangers the only way we know how to survive. This can never work, and eventually, our existence will collapse, along with our life.

The need for acknowledgment goes through all of our needs, no matter what they are, and the question is where it shows up the most.

The pain will eventually grow to the point that you will try to numb it somehow. You will need to step out from the chaos within. Your life will also fail, as it will never work with this approach. You need peace from the pain, something to get away from it.

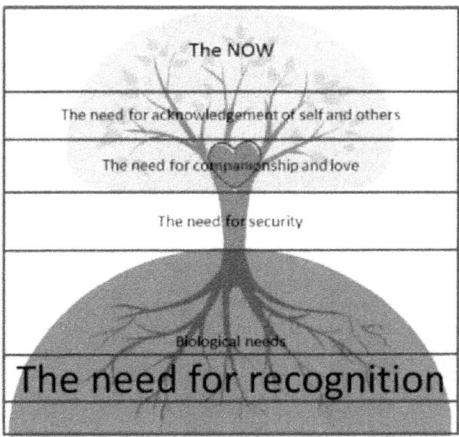

Figure 15: The Biological Threat

The possible behavioral consequences of this situation are:

Eating Disorders

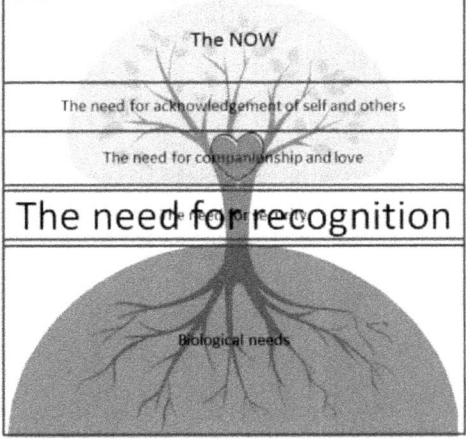

Figure 16: Risk-Needy

The possible behavioral consequences of this situation are:
  Risk-taking behaviors
  Self-harm

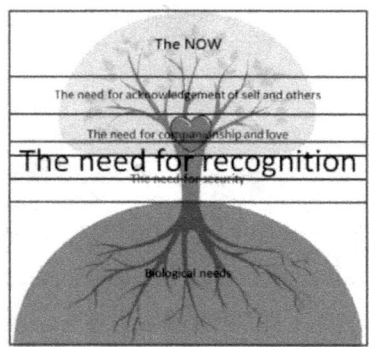

Figure 17: Love-, Sex-, Risk-Needy

The possible behavioral consequences of this situation are:
  Being acknowledged through sex
  Risky sexual behavior

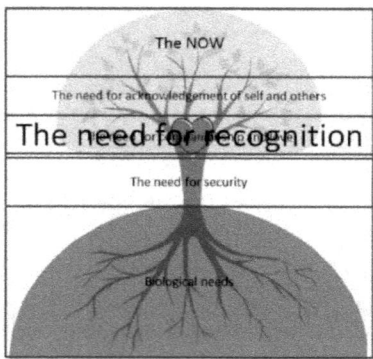

Figure 18: Love- or Sex-Needy

The possible behavioral consequences of this situation are:

    Interpreting kindness as love

    Interpreting sex as love

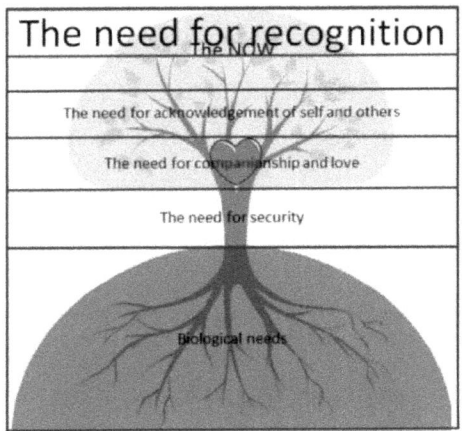

Figure 19: Socially Needy

The possible behavioral consequences of this situation are:

    Needing everybody to accept you, even strangers

    Being acknowledged by society

    Having power and influence

    Using and abusing mind impairment substances

    This tree will not survive.

If we put it all together in one picture, building from the base into the present, the picture might look like the one below. The only unknown variable is what goes into the area where the need for acknowledgment belongs, which depends upon individuals and situations. Yes, it can be a mess.

Nothing good comes out of this.

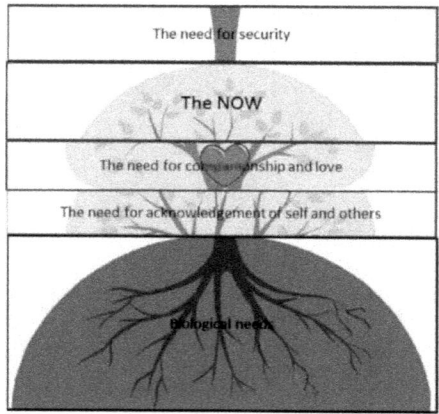

Figure 20: The Chaos Within

The Present Now

By working through our issues and using love and kindness to guide us, the picture changes. Little by little, the tree starts to correct itself. Life stops being controlled by dominating emotion. You start finding your way through life. It will become more balanced and in equilibrium with your authentic self.

I did it, and so can you.

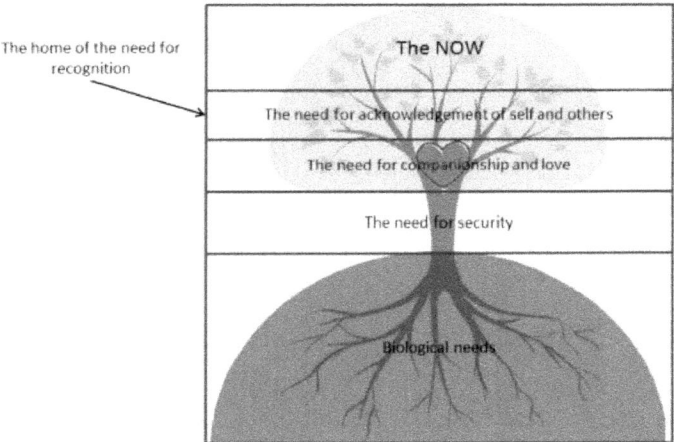

Figure 21: Today, after the Work

The possible behavioral consequences of this situation are:

Equilibrium in life, peace, and harmony—happiness

Understanding is key! Never lose focus on the fact that you are digging into the pain to find the wound and heal it, not to stay there forever! It is a process; trust the process. It will be *okay!*

Life is beautiful on the other side of the journey.

THE FORMULA FOR HAPPINESS

There is a formula for happiness that works!

Happiness = The Present minus Expectations

The Present, the Now

What is happening at this present moment?

The Present is always, in its way, good, solid, and meaningful. Sometimes it does not appear like that and does not make any sense. On some occasions, the Present that left us hurt, numb, and confused can take years to turn into a gift to our life.

Expectations

Suppose the index of Expectations is off the chart and has no bearing on reality. If so, then we will always be disappointed. The demand is that others are supposed to entertain us, fill us with their energy, and make us happy. Then we have a high number.

On the other hand, if you are grateful, honest about your emotions (then you are also honest with others), and entirely responsible for your life, then the index of Expectations will not flare up and expand. Then we have a low number.

The Outcome

If the strength of the Present is a higher number than the Expectations, then the outcome will be positive. I am happy.

If the strength of the Expectations is a higher number than the Present, then the outcome will be negative. The Present will be dull and not much fun. You cannot be happy if you are constantly disappointed.

What did I learn from this? If I take responsibility for myself and my actions, then the byproduct of this responsibility will be that I do not need others to fill my life with their energy. I will be at peace around others, and I will enjoy the Present. So, I am going to keep working on taking responsibility for myself in my life and use the index of Expectations to tell me where I am at each time!

EMOTIONAL VOLUME AND DANGEROUS PLACES

We can increase the volume of our emotional life every day, proportionally to our work and effort in improving ourselves during this journey. Little by little, we create more and more room for these strange things called feelings and emotions. We get better and better and stronger and stronger in dealing with what enters our lives, whether it is this issue or that issue. We get increasingly better at dealing with ourselves, more robust and stronger, more capable, happier and happier.

There are, however, things that could rock our boat so much that it might capsize. There are dangerous places on our journey, but if we are conscious and build a sound support system around us, we will reduce the risk considerably. If we know about dangerous places, we can face them with strength and love when they show up.

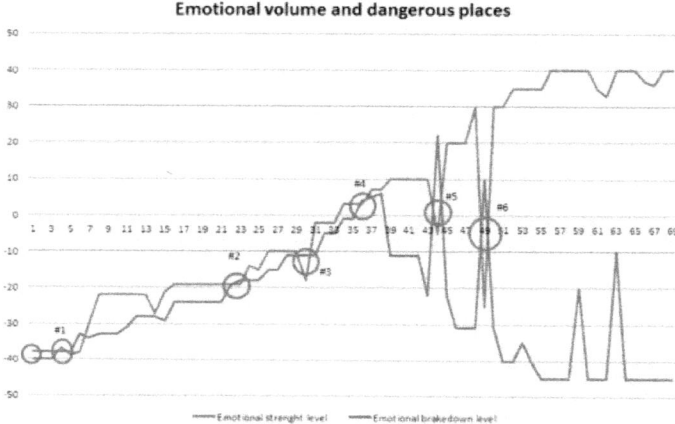

Figure 22: Emotional Volume and Dangerous Places

Figure 22 shows our emotional volume during the process. Our emotional volume is created between our Breaking Point and the height of our Emotional Abilities. In between those two points, we have our emotional volume, meaning the space where we can move around emotionally. Our Breaking Point determines how much negativity we can tolerate in our life at any given time. It is our bottom where we might break. Under certain conditions, our Emotional Volume is less than our Breaking Point, which is a dangerous state to be in. In that state, we have the danger of not wanting to continue this journey of life as we might feel that it is too difficult. It will pass. You just need to wait a little bit, hang on to something kind and loving, people, your child, your pet; find the light of kindness, and stay there until it passes.

Working on what you know is positive and builds you up. I have been there, and so have many others. You will be all right, it will pass, and life will improve significantly. You will look back on those moments in horror and joy simultaneously having gotten through them. Everything is possible; that, I know. There is only one thing that is not allowed during this process, and that is giving up. It will be all right; I believe in you!

Let's dig a little bit into the details.

The initial state:

The reason why we have not taken our own life before taking on the journey to recovery is very simple. We are shut down emotionally; we are in a mental coma state. There is no one home. No one is home in our emotional body. I was so efficient at it that I could disconnect myself with very short notice. It was so automatic that it occurred without my noticing. I would just disappear into the void without realizing it. We often think about suicide and how we should do it. In this place, it is our so-called flaws—for example, our emotional disconnection—that may actually keep us alive.

I was disconnected from the child within me until I started my healing journey. At the same time, the disconnection was making sure that the present me did not know too much because I, in the current Now, would not have handled it. To be full of the pain and have no tools or support to process it is a very dangerous place to be in.

When the need to self-destruct comes over us, we must not take it seriously. It is not a factbased condition. It is based on a false alarm. It comes from the pain within us that we cannot get rid of. We do not know how to get rid of it since we do not have the tools or solutions to deal with it. The pain will go away by working through it. There is only one thing that we may not do, and that is to give up.

When the need to selfdestruct visited me during this journey, I told it I was busy and that I would talk to it when I was finished working through my issues. It hung around me, trying to get attention, but eventually left. I am still here today, happy, and glad that I worked through these states of my mind.

Dangerous Places in Life

In the drawing, there are examples of dangerous situations that can come up in our journey toward our true life. Those are places where people are in real danger of taking their own lives. I do not think it is limited to these issues in the examples. There is always a way out of the pain, even though we cannot see it at these moments. The safe word is usually **Mobile Phone**, i.e., call someone, go to someone, or do something to get yourself out of that situation. Find the answers! They are out there. We just need to find them. When I have been at my worst, I read a clip hanging on my fridge. I still have it there more than twelve years later.

Words of Wisdom

"I believe in the sun, even when it isn't shining. I believe in love and kindness, even when it is not present. I believe in God, even when I cannot see him."

—Written on a cellar wall in the Jewish District in Warsaw, Poland

If this person could believe that there was something good in this world, then I can do that too. It does not matter how bad things seem to be. There is always light and love, though we cannot see them at the moment. The answers are inside of me. I just need to find them. Find something that fits you, something that takes you out of the emotional vortex zone. Love and kindness conquer all.

First Interception: Rewiring the Emotions

Here we have disconnected one wire in the emotional off switch, part of our old survival pattern, and connected one wire in the emotional on switch. We are opening up and connecting ourselves. We are not as good anymore at turning off our emotions, and we do not have the same control over the new survival tools to get away from the pain. We do not have our old foundation anymore and have not fully learned to handle the new one. We are actually making progress. The issue is that we have not started trusting the new tools fully, and the old tools do not work as well as they did before. We might have to make a leap of faith over to the new tools and hang on to them though we do not fully trust them. It will be okay. Just hang in there!

Second Interception: Thinking About Telling Your Family

This situation might arise when you think about telling your family about everything that happened. You might feel so much inner turmoil that you cannot do it. You might think that your family will hate you. That they will kick you out of their lives. You are actually rejecting yourself on behalf of others. Nobody can reject you but yourself. Remember, you are only thinking about it, not actually telling them. This phase is always a learning curve. Document what happened and keep it somewhere safe. You can work on it later, but these are valuable pieces of information. It will be okay! It will pass.

Third Interception: Informing Your Best Friend

We might be telling our best friend about what happened to us. We are opening ourselves to someone about everything, and let's say the individual does not know how to handle the information. Here we can have a very strange period, very conflicting. It will pass and be all right. Remember, what happened to you does not define you in any way. It just happened. You just happened to be there. You are in no way to be blamed for what happened!

Fourth Interception: Dealing with Embarrassment and Self-Shame

You are at a fairly good place in your life, and you are rising above the consequential behavioral patterns. This situation could come up when you think everybody knows that you are the victim of sexual violence. You might feel like you have a sign on your forehead stating, "I was raped," and you feel like it is there no matter where you go. You might be afraid that the people you work with or your social circle will discover what happened to you. You might be afraid of losing your job or status. This state of mind will pass, and it will be okay.

Fifth Interception: Telling Your Family for the First Time

This situation might arise when you finally tell your family about your abuse. Things might blow up, and the family will divide itself into groups. One group can be on your side. Another can be frozen in shock. They do not have the ability to deal with the situation. The third can get mad and go against you. To us, the second group falls into the third group, and we feel that they are against us because they do not take a stand with us.

You might even be physically abused, and no one will acknowledge your pain. This has nothing to do with you. It is theirs and theirs only. It is their emotional reaction to the information given, nothing else. Sometimes it is their own hidden trauma wounds that are screaming out and have nothing to do with you.

Things will work out. You can do it. I believe in you! It will be okay!

Sixth Interception: Telling Your Close Friends for the First Time

Here you might be telling your close friends for the first time. Your friends might tell you that you are no longer welcome in their homes, that you must not come near their children. This might occur because of the myth that victims become abusers. You might be faced with the line, "If you come near my children, I will kill you." You are thrown out, exiled, and dirtier than all things dirty. You might be attacked by madeup accusations, or the abuser will kill himself or herself, and the people in the community will blame you and attack you because of that. This thought of ending your life does not come from guilt or shame, but because you might ask: "My Higher Power, what is the point of this life? I have gone through hell trying to feel better and get my life back. Then these things come into my life, and they have nothing to do with me. What is the point of this life?" You might feel like you are facing the second round of hell all over again.

It is not your fault. People sometimes find it challenging to handle the ugliness that follows the truth. We are all in different places. It will pass. The world is full of wonderful people who are waiting to become your friend. You will be okay! We are alive! We got through it, and so can you! I believe in you!

ACTS OF VIOLENCE AND THEIR ENVIRONMENT

Being a victim of violence often leads to more violence when we speak up about it. In some cases, there are threats of violence, mockery, and isolation of the victim and her or his family to keep them from speaking out.

Below is a list of some of the factors that can be in the lives of victims of sexual violence and their families. This is what really happened and happens. It seems there is a lack of knowledge and understanding of these issues, especially in the court system. It is not just us, the victims of violence, that experience violence because of these issues, but also our families and friends. This is self-explanatory.

Sexual abuse and the environmental factors of victims and their families

Family

Loved ones

Children

Closest environment (Friends, neighborhood, closest communities)

Job

Sexual abuse victims / Acts of violence

Physical abuse

Loss of freedom

Rape, invasion of the body

Physical consequences

Emotional consequences

Threats of violence to maintain silence

Violence to maintain silence

Silence

Exclusion from families

Destruction of family

The urge to self-destruct

Bullying

Prejudice

Issues at work

Sexual abuse / Loved ones of victims / Acts of violence

Emotional exclusion

Exclusion from families

Destruction of family

Threats of violence to maintain silence

Violence to maintain silence

Bullying

Prejudice

Silence

ADDICTION, ADDICTS, OR IS IT SOMETHING ELSE?

Addiction, addicts—what is that? These are probably two of the most objectified words of today. They are something that no one wants to be subjected to. But what is it, really? Some people say, "Why doesn't he/she stop drinking, doing drugs, doing whatever? Why do they want this?" It is sometimes presented as someone who likes it and that it makes somebody happy.

Addiction is often defined by our society by the substance in use. What is your drug of choice? Maybe that is where the misunderstanding lies—defining addiction from the stuff the individual is using. The stuff is just the tool at hand and has, in fact, nothing to do with the addiction. It is just a chemical, behavior, or process, a dead thing. There is nothing personal about it. It is a catalyst. A transporter of sedatives that has one purpose—to take away the pain that is unbearable. The pain that is stuck within the "addict" which the "addict" is stuck underneath. The pain from which he cannot free himself!

The "addict" is a beautiful human being who is trapped in an addictive state! An unbearable state of pain! That pain will not give any peace, mercy, or holiday, and that pain will not allow him or her to get away from the vortex of the excruciating pain. The individual will therefore do anything to get away from it, to reach peace, and to break up the tornado state that they are stuck in. Do not misunderstand our smiles; relief is a wonderful thing.

Most of the time, almost always, people tend to look down on the individual who "has" an addiction. That is so messed up! How can you look down on someone who is stuck in a painful situation that is killing them? We need to rethink this!!! We have been taught that those of us who are "normal" are better, and the addicts are thought of as losers. Who wants to be humiliated while in pain? We must ask ourselves the question: Are we actually kicking somebody who is already lying on the ground?

Drugs of choice, behavior, or process have been used to define addiction. The addict "concept" has been marketed by the transporting chemical, behavior, or process of pain relief. By what the addicts chose, they fell into what was in front of them so that they might have a break from the unbearable pain that is killing that individual! A human being! Someone's child! Someone's parent! Somebody's sister or brother! A beautiful individual having problems regarding reaching inner peace, no matter what he or she tries. The root of socalled "addictions" are all the same, just different sedative items may be in use. There is no difference in the roots behind the addiction when slightly different sociallyapproved sedatives are used: alcohol, prescription drugs, sex, cards, social work, volunteer work, work, sports, money, power, influence, or anything that brings the person mentally out of their current lives and brings them into another space where they get some vacation from the emotional state, from the pain—a virtual reality because the reality is unbearable. I see no difference in the sedative catalysts. No one sedative is better than the other. They all serve the same purpose, soothing severe internal pain. That is the main point and what we need to focus on. We should stop looking at the sedative and turn towards the individual, the beautiful person who is crushed under the socalled addiction, collapsing from the pain. We need to get them out of the water before they drown.

I believe that we need to go under the layer of the sedative and talk to the beautiful person underneath. The one with the pain needs help to heal from the pain so that there will be no need for the sedative. I have witnessed the need for the sedative disappear after the beautiful individual managed to find their wounds, process them, heal them, make them whole, connect with themselves, get to know their own emotions, become content with themselves, get to know themselves as a whole individual, love themselves, love their surroundings, people, and life, and the sedative became unnecessary. It is incredibly beautiful to witness people reaching individual freedom—the freedom to be individuals in their own lives, the fundamental of being happy and sustainable.

Then there is the body. Are there side effects from the sedative that was used? We have to respect that and free the body of it after or when the mind becomes free from the pain. We must remember that it is a technical problem, not a personal one.

Our society has many solutions aimed towards replacing the sedative with another one without touching on the trauma. They are Band-Aids and do not work in the long run. If we had really found a solution, then there would be no one living on the streets due to their "addiction." There would be no children worried about the weekend and no homes breaking up because of the "situation." There would be no secrets that some people strive to keep under the carpet. We would be free from "addiction," and there would be no "unbearable pain."

We must stop focusing on the external point of view and turn inward toward the real problem! What happened to that beautiful human being? What are her or his wounds? What happened to my child, my sibling, my partner, my friend, my parent, and my family member? We must remove the pain so that the transporting catalyst becomes unnecessary.

RESPONSIBILITY FOR THE EMOTIONAL RESPONSES OF OTHERS

Nobody can take responsibility for how others feel. Each and every one of us has to take responsibility for our emotional responses to everything that occurs in our lives. We are all somewhere in our journey with our emotional life and learning to apply it to life.

If we were responsible for the emotional responses of others, then political correctness is the only truth in the world. Our responses, as well as those of the people around us, are constantly changing according to everyone's understanding at each moment in time. We are all evolving in our cognitive abilities, and our emotional being is growing each day. Nobody knows what tomorrow will bring.

Just remember that it is abnormal to be normal. Normal is an average, a number. We are not numbers, we are human beings; we are a spectrum. Let's embrace that. It would be horrible if everybody were the same—rather boring!

BEFORE YOU TAKE ON THIS JOURNEY

This journey will provoke everything in your life. Not only will it awaken your emotions, but it will also take time to learn how to use them.

Here is an overview of the journey ahead. It is broken down into eatable slices in Equilibrium Today - Book 2 – Practical Tools for Equilibrium and Equilibrium Today - Book 3 – Recovery Workbook.

Your bodily functions come into play. You have been in fight, flight, or freeze mode for a long time.

There is a study that everybody should take a look at. Those who were affected by the content of the study are more likely to be victims of sexual abuse during childhood and later on in life.

This is the CDC-Kaiser Permanente adverse childhood experiences (ACE) study and is one of the largest investigations of childhood abuse, neglect, household challenges, and later-life health and well-being.

The CDC stands for Centers for Disease Control and Prevention. It is part of the United States Department of Health and Human Service. Here is a link to the study:

https://www.cdc.gov/violenceprevention/aces/about.html

What are adverse childhood experiences?

Information on adverse childhood experiences and their consequences is found on the following CDC web page:

https://www.cdc.gov/violenceprevention/aces/fastfact.html

Adverse childhood experiences, or ACEs, are potentially traumatic events that occur in childhood (0-17 years). For example:

- Experiencing violence, abuse, or neglect
- Witnessing violence in the home or community
- Having a family member attempt or die by suicide

Also included are aspects of the child's environment that can undermine their sense of safety, stability, and bonding, such as growing up in a household with:

- Substance use problems
- Mental health problems

- Instability due to parental separation or household members being in jail or prison

Please note the examples above are not a complete list of adverse experiences. Many other traumatic experiences could impact health and well-being, such as not having enough food to eat, experiencing homelessness or unstable housing, or experiencing discrimination.

ACEs are linked to chronic health problems, mental illness, and substance use problems in adolescence and adulthood. ACEs can also negatively impact education, job opportunities, and earning potential. However, ACEs can be prevented.

What are the consequences?

ACEs can have lasting negative effects on health, well-being in childhood, and life opportunities, such as education and job potential, well into adulthood. These experiences can increase the risks of injury, sexually transmitted infections, maternal and child health problems (including teen pregnancy, pregnancy complications, and fetal death), involvement in sex trafficking, and a wide range of chronic diseases and leading causes of death, such as cancer, diabetes, heart disease, and suicide.

ACEs and associated social determinants of health, such as living in under-resourced or racially segregated neighborhoods, can cause toxic stress (extended or prolonged stress). Toxic stress from ACEs can negatively affect children's brain development, immune systems, and stress-response systems. These changes can affect children's attention, decision-making, and learning.

Children growing up with toxic stress may have difficulty forming healthy and stable relationships. They may also have unstable work histories as adults and struggle with finances, jobs, and depression throughout life. These effects can also be passed on to their own children. Some children may face further exposure to toxic stress from historical and ongoing traumas due to systemic racism or the impacts of poverty resulting from limited educational and economic opportunities.

Take the ACE Quiz on NPR — And Learn What It Does and Doesn't Mean

An ACE score is a tally of different types of abuse, neglect, and other hallmarks of a rough childhood. According to the Adverse Childhood Experiences study, the rougher your childhood, the higher your score is likely to be and the higher your risk for later health problems. You can take the test below:

https://www.npr.org/sections/health-shots/2015/03/02/387007941/take-the-ace-quiz-and-learn-what-it-does-and-doesnt-mean

Years and decades in an intense state of the body can be harmful. The best thing that you can do for your overall health is to work on the wounds within. Breaking away from getting drawn into the fight, flight, and freeze state of mind will take you out of this intense state of being and in the end, you will feel much better. Contact your doctor if there are any abnormalities.

You might feel like you are being hit by a runaway train when memories emerge. It is okay; I and many others felt like that too. Grab the memories and write them down, not to sink into them, but to work with them in the process. Look at it like data collection necessary to climb up from the hole that you feel like you are stuck in. Take on the role of an investigating journalist, investigating your life.

If you are on medication, then talk to your doctor and tell him or her what journey you are about to take on. You need to monitor your situation better than usual. There are going to be fluctuations in your bodily state. Our body can respond to the emotional upset that can follow this work. Everything is connected.

If you are undergoing some therapy, talk to your therapist about the journey ahead when and if you are ready to do so.

If you are in a 12-step program, ensure you have all the phone numbers you might need, and keep the meeting schedules handy. If you have a sponsor, then let him or her know about the journey ahead, when and if you are ready to do so.

If you have somebody whom you can confide in, talk to that person, tell him or her what you are doing, and make sure that that person is available.

There will be issues that come up during this journey, and I recommend that you seek a professional therapist to help you with these issues without interfering with the process itself. If you are not ready to expose everything about what you are going through at the moment, then you can take individual issues to the therapist and work through them.

Keep in mind that during the journey, you will get drained once in a while. It takes a lot of energy when we are working on our emotional body. After all, the brain is the most energyabsorbing organ there is.

If you feel that everybody is better without you and you want to take your life, then tell that voice that you are busy and you will talk to it later. Call somebody! The voice is giving you false information. We love you! You are valuable!

I told mine: "Ingolfur, I am busy at the moment, and I will talk to you when I am finished going through these issues." Then I cut contact with that voice since I will not have violence in my life, no more, never, ever again.

Sometimes it hung around, but by every step I took, it gradually lost control over me.

If you are in a love relationship, then it is better to tell that special one that your emotional fluctuations have nothing to do with him or her. You can start with saying, "I am working on issues from the past that are and will make me absent and that has nothing to do with you." At some point it would be good to tell that special one where you are coming from. If that hits the fan, then you are better off alone.

It will help if you have some music or something that can soothe your state of mind or help you face challenges. Something that you can grab hold of in the present.

This process will start a chain reaction in all areas of your life, mentally and physically. You can experience great changes, also fluctuations, and we need to be responsible for ourselves in this state. It is a bit like the sky is full of black suns, trauma wounds that are taking up your entire life. The only light that is shining in your daily life is darkness. You will take them down, one by one, with love and kindness toward yourself as a weapon. The biggest one goes down first, then the others will emerge as the focus calls for. Your day will become brighter and brighter, and the darkness will fade away.

You need to remember one thing: what you are about to go through has nothing to do with the present and nothing to do with your situation today. If it does have something to do with the situation that you are in today, you need to get out of it. If you cannot take that step today, then you will gain the strength to do so by going through the process. It will be all right.

ADDITIONAL READING MATERIAL

The author's blog: https://equilibrium.today/

I recommend searching the Internet for everything that comes to mind. It is my hope that this book will give you a good start to your healing. It will give you one set of tools based on my knowledge and experience and methods that helped me and many others. But do not stop here. Keep an open mind and never stop learning. Each person is unique, and you need to build your own set of tools that work best for you, taking from the ones in this book and adding your own. My goal for your life is that you learn from me and get rid of me in the process, becoming strong, independent, free, authentic, happy, and self-sufficient in all aspects of your life.

ABOUT THE AUTHOR

Ingolfur Hardarson is an author and advocator who, as a child, endured sexual, physical, emotional, and mental abuse. He also experienced being bullied in his early years because of a medical condition related to his sexual abuse. When Ingolfur was in his forties, while working his way through a 12-step codependency program, he started gaining back some long-lost memories from his childhood which later prompted him to successfully work his way out of darkness into personal freedom.

After finding his way from the depths of despair up to the surface of everyday life, he published a book about his healing journey called *Ferðalag til frelsis (A Journey to Freedom)*. He has worked intensely with over 150 individuals in recovery from all sorts of abuse. He has also spent countless hours assisting relatives of abuse victims, as in his own words, "Everybody must work together." His blog is his way of paying it forward and ensuring that the methodology he developed through his own crisis will live on. Over 700 individuals have worked on their issues using this methodology to various extents.

Ingolfur has been in many interviews on national TV, radio, and newspapers as well as hosted a radio show for victims of violence. He has also written articles and assisted in constructing a TV show surrounding sexual abuse in Iceland.

Ingolfur has assisted in several research projects at the University of Iceland and the University of Akureyri. His motto is to do everything in his power to make sure that professionals gain a deeper understanding of the inner world of sexual abuse victims so that they be better equipped to help survivors.

"Truth guided by love and kindness conquers all. I have faith in you!

Have a pleasant journey." – Ingolfur Hardarson

UPCOMING BOOKS

Book 2

Book 3

For more info on these and upcoming books,
Visit https://equilibrium.today

www.ingramcontent.com/pod-product-compliance
Lightning Source LLC
Chambersburg PA
CBHW050109170426
43198CB00014B/2514